LOVE HARD

LOVE HARD

THE TRIUMPHANT STORY OF A MOTHER'S ROLLER COASTER RIDE OF LOVING AND PARENTING A CHILD WITH MENTAL HEALTH STRUGGLES.

DEBORAH MUELLER

MANUSCRIPTS
PRESS

COPYRIGHT © 2023 DEBORAH MUELLER

LOVE HARD

The Triumphant Story of a Mother's Roller Coaster Ride of Loving and Parenting a Child with Mental Health Struggles.

ISBN   979-8-88926-746-1   *Paperback*

979-8-88926-747-8   *Ebook*

To moms everywhere who feel exhausted,
overwhelmed, and hopeless. You are not alone.

CONTENTS

———

FOREWORD

It takes a strong, determined person to write a book about the raw and real struggles of raising a child with mental health challenges. It's not a fairytale with pretend characters and dialogue.

What is written in this book, *Love Hard*, is the truth. It's real life with no sugar-coating.

But it's also a love story.

I admit, at times, I struggled reading it. I have no memory of the hardest moments because of mania and blackouts. It's scary reading the damage you've caused or could've potentially caused yourself and your family. But that is nothing compared to what my mom and dad went through trying to protect their kids from the ugly parts.

That's probably why my mom almost didn't write this book.

You see, becoming an author is a long, difficult journey mixed with emotions of fear, anxiety, and excitement. Wanting your book to be the best, but at the same time also wondering who will judge you or judge your child. Debating if you are good enough to even write a book. I've seen my mom go through all of this.

But ultimately, and thankfully, she decided to sit down and just write about the lowest lows, highest highs, and everything in between. She stayed up late into the night, typed away at her computer, and turned down fun events or activities to write about our struggles. She did all this with a determination to help just *one* other mom.

While she was writing, I saw her laugh, cry, become flustered, and want to scratch the entire book and quit. But she didn't. That's not my mom. She always finishes what she starts. I know this because she didn't give up on me. A kid who didn't know how to stand up for herself. Hell, I might've given up on me. But through everything, she stood there by me, for me, and with me.

I certainly got lucky to have the mom I have. The model my mom set for me with her faith, work ethic, and determination have all been engraved in my head, and it pushes me to be the best I can be.

That's why *I want her to share this book* with the entire world. I want people to know our story. And for the people who know me, I want them to know the past and the dark so they can see me now, in the light. I want people to see my mom as the woman who kept going and worked her ass off as a mom and businesswoman. God has given her an incredible gift that she needs to use to give other mothers hope for better days and to see that success is truly possible.

I only pray that someday I'm half as good a mom as she is.

I love you, Momma.

Mia

INTRODUCTION

———

I met Holly in a hotel lobby while drinking wine. My youngest daughter and I were wrapping up the last few games of a summer filled with AAU (Amateur Athletic Union) basketball travel. Holly had a daughter playing in the same tournament but for a different team. A mutual friend introduced us, and we began an easy conversation. Jobs, husbands, kids… we clicked. Soon, we realized that in addition to our seventeen-year-olds, we each had a daughter in their twenties too. Mine would be graduating college that spring. After a few vague jokes about the difficulties my husband and I had raising her, I admitted that out of all my kids, she was never the one we imagined would finish in four years and also have a job lined up. I casually shared some of her struggles, proud of how far she'd come.

Holly looked at me with tears in her eyes and grabbed my forearms. "Deb, we were meant to meet," she said. It turned out she had her own hidden, messy, sometimes ugly parenting stories of raising a daughter with mental health issues too. My stories and my honesty allowed her a safe space to be open and vulnerable. In that moment, she was no longer alone in her struggle. We spent an hour talking and laughing with each other. We were amazed at the many goosebump moments we experienced as we realized the irony of our similarly strained parenting journeys, which is when I felt God's push. If my story could offer hope, healing, less loneliness, and inspiration to just one other mom, then I needed to write about it.

My story? The roller-coaster ride that includes loving and parenting a child who struggles with mental health. I know firsthand how hard it is to raise a child with mental health issues. I know the affects it has on your marriage, your family, and your own mental health. I've spent sixteen years believing in, fighting for, and protecting my daughter. My intent has always been to help her understand and believe she was not a mistake or bad kid. She was simply wired differently. My intent was to find ways for her to live with and manage her struggles and not let her struggles define or limit her.

If you search "stigma" on Google, the dictionary definition at the top of the search results from Oxford Languages is "a mark of disgrace associated with a particular circumstance, quality, or person." If you then search "stigma example" on Google, the first site to load is sadly, "Stigma, discrimination, and mental illness." Although the perception of mental illness has improved over the years, there is still a powerful negative stigma that exists. I've heard that one in four Americans will be affected by a mental health disorder in any given year, and many more will have a family member affected. It's imperative that the world hears more stories and becomes more educated so that those who are struggling can be better supported and accepted.

Let me put it out there, I am not a registered doctor of anything. I am a mom who put in years of love, discipline, therapy, sweat, and a heck of a lot of tears. That's my qualification. And I know not every parent and child relationship will have a successful outcome when mental illness exists. I know some moms give all of themselves, and their child remains stuck, never finding the solutions they desperately need. I also sadly know some children are lost to mental illness forever. But when I was in the deepest pits of parenting and felt alone, lost, exhausted, frustrated, helpless, and wanted to give up on my kid—or believed she'd be better off with a different mom because I was surely screwing everything up—I needed hope. And that's what my story offers.

Hope and encouragement to keep going, to look deeper for help, to ask the difficult questions, to give grace, and to speak up. And also, the inspiration that it might get better and easier. Success stories are out there, and you could very well be one.

This book is based on my memories, interviews with family members, and written records. I changed the names of certain people who appear in the book to preserve their anonymity or because I was unable to reach them for their consent. I'm not sure how much of what we tried will be helpful to other parents, but we did our best. I've included resources, which I recently found and wished they had been available to me at the time. And I know there is no single right answer, nor a clear road map, for families of those struggling with mental health. But, in our story, I hope some solace can be found, some guidance, and, if nothing else, some company.

I am not alone, which is proven each time I come across another mom like Holly, who knows and owns the struggle. We feel like failures at times, but we are so far from it. We are on the front lines of advocacy for someone we love struggling with mental health. We need to hear stories of solidarity but also hope. Stories that make us, for a brief moment, feel ordinary and heard. Stories that normalize instead of ostracize.

To the woman who's exhausted, feels alone, overwhelmed, is fighting, and has a story but can't or won't share it to protect those she loves. I see you. I hear you. I know you.

The road is rough, but it can be navigated. Love hard.

CHAPTER ONE

We are never in control. Even in the moments when we feel we are the most. All you can do is work hard, throw yourself into the deep end, believe the impossible is possible, and then close our little peepers and take a leap of faith. Like Indiana Jones, I've found that the bridge shows up sturdy under my feet every time, even when it takes me to a destination I wasn't anticipating.

—ALEXIS JONES

I hate roller coasters, and I always have.

It's 1990, and I'm at an amusement park with friends. They promise me I'll be fine. It'll be fun. How do I know I won't love it unless I try it? I go on two rides. They're both terrifying. They both leave me feeling sick and shaky. I am content sitting on benches while my friends continue riding the rest of the day.

Fast-forward to 1998. I am at a church festival with my husband and his daughter. They ask me to go on the tilt-a-whirl with them. It's been some years, I am older, and maybe I will finally like rides. I say okay. But when the door shuts us in, I am acutely aware of the heat, the smell of sweat and cotton candy, the hardness of the curved wall I'm leaning on, and the nervous energy of the riders alongside me. When we start to slowly spin, I panic. As we pick up speed, I close my eyes and pray I don't get sick and the ride will end. I vow to never go on another ride in my life.

The source of my anxiety is the unknown and lack of all control. I don't like the gradual climbs followed by rocketing plummets. I don't like the stomach flips I get with the spinning and twisting, flying, and lurching along a metal track. I don't appreciate the suspense. I fear the highs and dread the drops. Of course, this is why God would see it fitting to gift me with a strong-willed, or "spicy," child and strap us in beside each other on the emotional roller-coaster ride of our lives.

Our journey began in the womb when we required a Flight-for-Life helicopter ride during Thanksgiving weekend of 1999. And this led to seemingly endless nights of colic, night terrors, and bouts of anxiety. Our ride continued through a sixteen-year struggle with the ups and downs of mental health. There were periods of time when the track seemed to level out, be enjoyable and fun while relatively calm, and times when things were completely out of control and terrifying. Parenting my daughter was never predictable and often unconventional. But as much as that made it challenging, I found it also made it remarkable.

My daughter was truly a gift. Her conception very intentional—not a fun roll in the hay and oops, I got pregnant. My husband, Gary, and I tried for an entire year before getting some preliminary testing done to make sure all the pipes were clean, swimmers healthy, and eggs present. Things initially looked discouraging, but, as it's been known to happen, the very month we discovered possible complications was the same month we conceived. And so began my fairly textbook pregnancy.

That is, until month eight. On our annual trip to northern Wisconsin to spend a weekend with my in-laws, I started bleeding. Friends who've been pregnant, you might remember two things: (1) you have to pee all the time, especially at night during the third trimester, and (2) the "climate" down below is closer to the aviary exhibit at the zoo, almost sauna-like. When you get up to pee, it's not uncommon to already feel slightly wet. But when there's blood pooling in the toilet, you instantly know something is wrong.

"Gary, I need to call the doctor. I'm bleeding."

These are words no husband wants to be woken up with. I was amazingly calm. I assessed the problem, called the doctor's office for the OB on call—miraculously mine—and then called her at home.

"Hi Deb, what's going on?" my doctor asked, still slightly groggy as I had just woken her up.

After I explained I was bleeding and what time it started, she asked, "Have you had intercourse lately? Is there cramping? Do you feel any contractions?"

I replied no to all three questions. At that point, I handed the phone to Gary because the wad of toilet paper I'd placed in my underwear had already soaked through and needed to be replaced.

"I'd like you to take her to the hospital immediately. If you can make it, there's a new, very reputable one about an hour from you, and they'll call me when you arrive. If on the way, the bleeding gets heavier or is accompanied by cramping or contractions, stop at the first hospital you pass," the doctor told my anxious husband.

"What's going on?" asked my concerned father-in-law after he heard us on the phone.

"Deb started bleeding. Her doctor wants me to get her to the hospital, and we need to leave right away." Gary was focused, but I could hear the worry in his voice.

"Let me get dressed, and I'll go with you. You shouldn't do this alone," my mother-in-law offered.

I changed, packed a small bag, and headed to the truck. It was still dark outside as they helped me lie down in the back seat and elevate my legs. A ride that normally took an hour and fifteen minutes went by in thirty-nine minutes. Gary was almost hopeful we'd get pulled over so he could get a police escort and get there even sooner.

"How are you doing?" Gary asked as we neared the first hospital on the way.

I hadn't felt much blood, so I said, "Keep going. I think we can make it."

He continued to check on me periodically while my mother-in-law made small talk, keeping Gary company and focused.

I remember lying on the back seat praying for a sign my baby was okay, and the wave of relief I felt when he or she finally moved. Although everything felt surreal, my panic and alarm still held at bay, I said many prayers of thanks and silently continued to encourage my baby to hang on.

When we arrived at the hospital, I was seated in a wheelchair and taken to the emergency admitting department and then to a room on the labor and delivery floor. Now that I was sitting up, the bleeding had intensified, so I was anxious to lie down in bed.

"Hi, Deborah. I'm the nurse who will be handling your care. I'd like to go over your case. It says you're thirty-two weeks pregnant, bleeding since 6 a.m., you're from the Milwaukee area, and this is your first baby. I also see noted that your twenty-week ultrasound did show a low-lying placenta, and you are scheduled for a follow-up ultrasound to be done in five days to check its positioning. Until now, you've had no spotting or problems," she verified. During that conversation, additional nurses worked to get an IV started, take blood samples, hook me up to a fetal monitor, check on my bleeding, and take my vitals.

About an hour and a half later, I was able to meet the local doctor of the hospital. She ordered an in-room ultrasound.

It showed most of the placenta was exactly where it was supposed to be, but a piece similar to a tail had slipped down along the side of my uterus and was covering 75 percent of my cervix, which was the opening my baby was supposed to deliver through. This is also referred to as partial placenta previa. The concern in cases of placenta previa is that "as your cervix opens during labor, it can cause blood vessels that connect the placenta to the uterus to tear, which can lead to bleeding and put both you and your baby at risk. Women who have this condition will have to have a C-section to keep this from happening" (WebMD Editorial Contributors 2022).

Midafternoon, my parents called me. That's when, after all the hours of stress and activity, I lost it. My chest tightened, my lips quivered, and I felt the pressure of unshed tears behind my eyes at the sound of my dad's voice. I don't even remember what was said, but I was so choked up, I couldn't talk.

Next, my mom got on the phone. "Deb, should we come? I want to be there with you," her voice full of love and concern. She wanted to be with me so badly, but we had no idea what the next twenty-four hours held. It didn't make sense for them to start a five-hour drive if I would ultimately be moved.

"No, it's okay. Not yet, I'm just so happy to talk to you. I'm so scared, Mom, and there's so much going on," my voice shook with insecurity and a longing for the woman who always made things better.

Around this same time, though the bleeding was slowing down, it had triggered contractions, and they were coming fairly regularly. The fear was that my cervix would react and start dilating, and I'd go into labor. I was given the first of what would end up being three steroid shots to aid in the development of my baby's lungs. If I delivered early, then this would give him or her a better chance of breathing on their own. They also started me on a drug called magnesium sulfate. The doctor explained they had put it off as long as they felt was possible, but they needed to stabilize the ongoing contractions. This drug was basically a muscle relaxer, and they hoped it would relax my uterus enough to stop the contractions. It was not harmful to my baby in the long term, but if I did deliver, the baby would be lethargic and "floppy."

The side effects of magnesium sulfate were horrible. I ended up needing the highest dose available, which caused terrible nausea, headache, dry mouth, and double vision. My body was on fire. I could not talk coherently. If I moved my head, the room swam. I could not sleep because my mind was racing. I was not allowed to eat in case an emergency C-section was necessary. I was put on a catheter because the drug prevented me from sensing a full bladder, and a full bladder could cause my contractions to intensify. By the evening, the contractions had slowed, and it was decided I needed to be moved. Though this hospital was new and reputable, it was not equipped to deliver a preemie baby, which was still a very real possibility.

Gary was a rockstar. He was always reassuring and present. He was worried about our baby but also about me, and my pain caused him pain. Overnight, he listened to all the nurses, the local doctor, and my OB. He factored in all the events we'd been through and the predictions for what might come.

The next morning, Gary ran out to get boxes of thank-you donuts for the incredible nurses who stayed through their shift end to see my case through. It was decided that the most efficient way to get me to a hospital that could better handle my care and was closer to home was by Flight-for-Life helicopter. An ambulance ride would've taken too long and didn't have enough room for the equipment I required. The local charter plane declined by saying too much could go wrong in the two and half hours it would take to get me to Milwaukee.

"It's Sunday, there's no way to check insurance to see how much this will cost and if it's covered," one of the nurses reminded us.

"First priority is getting Deb home. We'll find a way," was Gary's reply.

And our family immediately agreed, offering to help us financially, if necessary, but wanting to get me home. In the end, and thanks to the blessing of good insurance coverage, we were not charged a dime for that ride of a lifetime.

The Flight-for-Life crew arrived at 9:30 a.m. and transferred me from the bed to a gurney. Then, they hurried to disconnect me from the hospital's tubes and monitors and reconnect me to their equipment—two IVs, one sensor on my back, two on my chest, and one on my index finger. Through nervous tears of gratitude, we said quick goodbyes to this amazing group of hospital staff. These people were only in my life for a little over twenty-four hours, but they left a lasting impression and are still incredibly special to me. As I was loaded into the helicopter, I was able to give Gary a quick kiss goodbye. There was only room for the pilot and two crew members, so he would be driving the five hours home alone. I held his hand a second longer than usual, memorizing the strength and reassurance I saw reflected in his eyes. So much could happen in the time we'd be apart, and I was terrified. I tried to focus more on the fact that I was stabilized and headed closer to home. My flight made it to Milwaukee in an hour and fifteen minutes, forty minutes ahead of schedule because of a strong tailwind, and landed at a small local airport, where I was taken by ambulance to the hospital.

I spent eight days in the hospital, mostly in bed being monitored. I passed the days watching TV, journaling, reading, playing games, and visiting with the family and friends who often came by. I would get stir-crazy, but at the same time, I felt safe knowing there was a staff of professionals taking care of me. I had ultrasounds done that confirmed and officially diagnosed me with partial placenta previa. This diagnosis meant that my original birth plan was no longer an option. Doctors recommended I proceed with a Cesarian section, also commonly known as a C-section. The baby would now be delivered "through surgical incisions made in the abdomen and uterus" (Mayo Clinic Staff 2022) versus my previous plan for vaginal delivery. I was given strict bed rest orders for the remainder of my pregnancy and needed to stay within a fifteen-minute car ride of the hospital in case I had a spontaneous bleed again. The only place suitable was my parent's house.

This new twist in our pregnancy required a major pivot. Not only for me, but for my wonderfully flexible and tolerant parents who went from empty nesters to full-time parents again overnight. They were to share their home with not just me but my friends and family for the remaining weeks of my pregnancy, which was looking to be close to two months. But also, for Gary. When Gary was twenty, he got married and had a baby girl. His marriage only lasted a couple of years, but the day he became a father for the very first time changed who he was forever. He became a better version of himself. The way he completely and unconditionally loved his daughter was one of the many reasons I fell madly in love with him years earlier. His daughter—my bonus daughter—was now fourteen. She lived with her mom, which was forty-five minutes from us, and had a pretty active social and athletic calendar, as most teens do. He coached her in sports and spent every other weekend with her, which was the norm in custody agreements back then. So now, he had to split his time between work, our home that still needed to be managed, his daughter's world and activities, and my parent's home, me, and all our appointments. I don't know how he did it, but he never complained, he always showed up, and I was so incredibly grateful.

For those last two months, the only time I was out of my parents' house was to go to doctor's appointments. They became dates with Gary that I craved. I got to wear shoes and do my hair. We were out in public around people. We had some one-on-one time on the car ride there and back. I assume my mom enjoyed the freedom too, because all other times I was at home, I required around-the-clock "babysitting." My parents had to find someone to sit with me if they wanted to leave the house just in case I needed an unexpected and immediate ride to the hospital.

I handled bedrest fairly well in the first few weeks. But toward the end, it was more with the dignity of an overtired toddler being told "no" in the candy aisle of the grocery store. My mom was a saint. I sulked and whined about missing Christmas at my house and my own baby shower. I was becoming irritated at the constant monitoring. "What are you doing? Why are you up? Sit down. Shouldn't you stay off your feet?" All appropriate questions and said with love, but man, I was missing the world outside of the four walls of my parent's house. I wanted to decorate our Christmas tree with Gary and his daughter. I wanted to go downhill skiing with them and shop at the mall. I didn't want to be stuck playing board games on the millennium New Year's Eve. I wanted to be out at a party. My mom had every right to scream at me for being a spoiled brat raining on her daily parade and remind me this was no picnic for her either, but she was patient and just kept loving me while giving me space to wallow.

It wasn't ideal for anyone, but for the sake of this baby who we had all already fallen in love with, we sucked it up and did the damn thing. I look back now, and I appreciate the time I spent being my parent's little girl before becoming a parent myself. And I appreciate the adjustments they made to accommodate me.

Finally, it was the date of my scheduled C-section. One week early but totally out of any danger. It was time to meet our baby, find out if it was a boy or girl, and get both of us out of any possible danger.

"Let's stop at the gas station and grab a paper with the date on it to commemorate our baby's birthday," Gary said on our early morning drive to the hospital. I loved the idea. I loved his excitement. Our hospital check-in went smoothly, as did the prep in our room. It was finally go time! When it was time, I was wheeled to the operating room doors where Gary kissed me. He said, "I'll see you soon," and left to get prepped for surgery himself. Once inside the room, my stomach was washed and sterilized, and a spinal block was administered while I listened to Enya playing in the background per my doctor's request. Gary arrived in his scrubs. His eyes literally danced with anticipation and joy.

It was all so surreal that after thirty-nine weeks of wondering, praying, and dreaming, our entire world would change in a matter of minutes. I felt tugging and pulling. I heard the murmurs of doctors, focused and professional. I continually asked Gary for updates as he could see over the sterile screen they'd set up. Suddenly, I heard a cry—a miraculous, resounding, angry wail. And all was so good. It was a girl, and she was healthy. The doctor held her up so I could get my first glimpse of this scrunchy, red-faced, beautiful human, and then she cut the cord. I watched as a nurse took her to the warmer to get cleaned up, weighed, and measured. Gary went to clamp the remainder of the cord and watch as she pinked up and had her tiny footprints inked. After she was swaddled, he brought her over so I could study my new baby. She was perfect.

But in a matter of seconds, what had been a calm room turned frenzied, and the attention was back on me. There was blood—too much blood. My doctor didn't know where it was coming from, which meant she didn't know how to stop it. Gary quickly handed the baby back to the nurses and grabbed my hand. He watched with concern as they moved organs out of the way and dug deeper into my abdomen cavity to locate the bleed. I saw fear in his eyes. I heard it in the doctor and nurses' hushed conversation. It took minutes—very long and intense minutes—to find the source of bleeding and stop it. I couldn't feel anything or see anything, but I felt light-headed and nauseous from anxiety and loss of blood. Gary stayed by me until the surgery was back under control. Then they asked him to go with our daughter to the nursery where he could show her to our family, who had been waiting to meet her. I laugh because I remember him being torn for a minute. Wanting to go with his new baby but pulled to also stay with his wife. After he and our baby left and the doctors finished closing me up, I was wheeled to a recovery room where I could finally call my close friends and excitedly share that our baby, Mia, had been born, and we were both happy and healthy.

A healthy, textbook pregnancy turned high-risk and unpredictable. A planned, well-orchestrated delivery encountered a potentially life-threatening glitch. It was an appropriate beginning to the roller coaster that would be life with our daughter in the days and years to come.

CHAPTER TWO

Being a parent is like folding a fitted sheet. No one really knows how.

—UNKNOWN

Do you hold a sheet by the two adjacent corners of one of the shorter edges and with the sheet inside out, place a hand in each of those two corners? Do you begin by laying the sheet flat with the corners facing in and the elastic edge facing up? Or do you roll the thing up into a ball and shove it into the closet? Perhaps, there is a most commonly practiced way of folding a fitted sheet, but no one way can truly be deemed the best or most correct. The bottom line is we choose a method, adapt as needed, and do our best. The same goes for parenting. It is not a one-size-fits-all job. Depending on your child, your beliefs, and your family dynamic, you are allowed to choose the style that works for you and then adapt if necessary.

Our C-section delivery wasn't what I had envisioned when I got pregnant, nor was it what I had initially prepared for. But in the end, it was our success story, and I embraced it. I rode the roller-coaster ride of our pregnancy journey, learning over forty weeks it was impossible to avoid the highs and lows. I focused on managing the surprises while embracing the moments of joy and excitement.

According to the Cleveland Clinic, "Most people will spend two to four days in the hospital after a C-section. During this time, the hospital staff will help with pain management, ensure you're eating and drinking enough and help you move around. This is all in addition to bonding with your newborn, which can include attempting to breastfeed" (Higgins 2021). I ended up staying an additional night after developing a migraine caused by the spinal block. Mia stayed with me during the day, but every evening, the nurses took her to the nursery so I could sleep and heal, only bringing her back to me to nurse every four hours.

Let's talk about breastfeeding. Kudos to those who do it, and I support all mamas in any way they deem fit to feed their babies. Over time, it ended up being really wonderful, but initially, I struggled. It was weird and hard. I chose to try it, but I wasn't prepared for how unnatural it initially felt. Literally overnight, my boob became a vessel of nourishment. A human being latched on to it and sucked so hard I'd grimace in excruciating pain, and tears would come to my eyes. It was painful! Cracked nipples and engorgement were very unpleasant surprises after what I'd read and heard in classes about how nursing would be the most natural and special experience I'd have with my baby. I was incredibly grateful for those extra days in the hospital with access to lactation consultants and nurses. They reassured me and patiently taught us how to find positions and a routine that worked. They also helped me with pain relief.

I flowed through each day in a fog. First from the pain medication and then from the whirlwind of daily activity that made days pass quickly. If it wasn't hospital staff coming in to check on me, take vitals, get me up walking, or check on my baby, it was friends and family coming to visit. Gary went back to work but spent evenings with me, the bright spot in my days. He looked forward to seeing us and was always willing to change a diaper, bathe, burp, or hold Mia. He brought his fourteen-year-old daughter to visit a number of times, too, making sure she felt part of our growing family and equally important.

On day five of my stay, I was given the all clear to go home, and I was presented with our discharge paperwork. Gary and his daughter came in the morning to get us, my belongings, and the many flowers, gifts, and extra baby supplies we'd accumulated since our delivery. I was sore and bleeding. I still had a dull headache from my migraine the day before. And I was secretly terrified. I was scared to go home. Independence suddenly overwhelmed me. My baby scared me. How would I know if I was doing things right without anyone there to monitor me? Who would reassure and help me? I spent two months relying on everyone else and being taken care of day and night. Now, I would actually be on my own again but with a baby. I was out of practice and had lost all confidence in my abilities to handle life.

"She's so small. She doesn't even fit in this car seat! Can she breathe? She's so smooshed. I'm just going to sit in the back with her to make sure she's breathing," I anxiously said to Gary as we loaded her into the car. On the ride home, I watched my new baby girl. Every little noise I found cute in the hospital now made me fearful. Was her breathing labored because her head was slumped forward? Was that quiet gurgle the sound of her choking?

"Why is everyone driving so fast?" Gary nervously said from the front seat. "I never noticed until I had a new baby in the back seat of the car how many idiots are on the road! Everyone needs to slow down!"

As we pulled up to the house, there were signs and balloons welcoming us home. After being on bedrest at my parents' house for two months, it was a sight for sore eyes. And when I looked at Gary, I saw a face filled with excited expectations for our life ahead. He finally had his family home—under one roof. A healthy wife and now two beautiful daughters. Life was good! So why did I feel like crying? Why did I feel panic in my chest? I was supposed to be incredibly happy and grateful too. Instead, I felt this self-imposed pressure to play a role I no longer felt at all prepared for. I felt like an imposter. How was I a mom who was responsible for a tiny human? How in the hell did I get here seemingly so quickly when really, the past two months had crawled by? Before I could self-destruct, some of our family came to visit. A distraction that temporarily saved me from having an emotional meltdown.

As the day rolled into evening, and while our family was still keeping me company, Gary left to take his oldest daughter back home to her mom's house. Those who stayed back with me continued holding and attending to Mia. She was content, and I was grateful for the extra hands as my C-section incision was sore from the day's extra activity. Dinner was made, and then the dishes were done. After Gary returned home, our guests said it was time to go. They said quick goodbyes, thank-yous, and gave kisses. For the first time, it was just the three of us alone.

Gary and I watched some TV. At around 9 p.m., he kissed me goodnight and went upstairs to bed. I stayed up to breastfeed Mia and "take in" the house that I had been gone from for so long. At around 10 p.m., with her sound asleep, I laid Mia in the cradle next to our bed, brushed my teeth, washed my face, and got into bed. That's when the unstoppable tears started. I was sobbing and couldn't stop. I was immediately scared. Her little breaths sounded so loud. Was something wrong? What if they stopped? And was she warm enough? Or too cold? Had she eaten enough? What if she died? I already loved her so much. How would I survive? She was so tiny and fragile. I was completely overwhelmed with my daughter and all that came with now having her—the responsibility, the intense love. I felt alone even though my husband was sound asleep right next to me. I missed the security of my mom and her house.

Snot and tears doused my face as I worked to quiet the sobs racking my body. After about twenty minutes of my emotional breakdown, Gary woke up from his restful sleep to my ugly, snotty, sniveling-lip hysterics. And, of course, his initial thought was that something had happened to Mia. Being logical when, for me, logic was clearly out the window. It took him a minute to wake up enough to grasp the idea that nope, it was just me being really, really sad while our baby girl was sleeping soundly next to our bed in her cradle.

"What's wrong? Did something happen to Mia?" Gary asked, panicking when he saw me crying.

"No, it's me," I whispered shakily. "I feel so much love, but I'm also so scared, and I don't want to be alone. And I'm sad, and I don't know why, but I am. I need you to sit with me for a little bit downstairs."

And he did. He held me on our couch while I cried, neither of us really understanding why.

"I always assumed," Gary quietly said to the top of my head, "that I'd be up with a crying baby but never dreamed the baby would be sound asleep and I'd be up with my crying wife." Oh, how I loved that he showed up for his hot mess of a wife at that moment.

At my postpartum follow-up appointment, I was feeling better emotionally but still wanted to discuss the earlier anxiety and overwhelming sadness I had felt with my OB-GYN. She told me I had a case of "the baby blues, diagnosed as feelings of sadness in the first few days after having a baby. Up to four in five new parents (80 percent) have the baby blues, and they are common in women who are nervous about taking care of their new baby or worried about how their life has changed since the baby was born. They usually go away on their own, within a few days or up to two weeks" (March of Dimes 2021).

Bonding with my newborn daughter did not prove to be instant or come naturally for me either, which was an unexpected disappointment, adding to my feelings of inadequacy and making Mia all the more intimidating. All my life, I expected I'd settle into mothering as easily as I had babysitting. I loved kids, and they tended to love me back, so why should this be so different and hard? But because there had been so much distraction and extra attention given to Mia and me in the five days following her birth, I hadn't been forced to really mother her outside of breastfeeding. Between Gary, family, friends, and hospital staff, her needs were met while I sat in bed and watched.

So now, to be completely hands-on filled me with insecurity and panic. And insecurity and panic filled me with new-mom guilt. None of those were amazing emotions to experience as my hormones raged, and I was trying to adjust to my new role. So, I had to start over and connect with my daughter by being hands-on. I needed to learn from her cues and create our bond. Boy, was she a good teacher; I just had to survive some of her more difficult lessons.

The same night of my emotional collapse, Mia chose to cluster feed, which is "when your baby wants to nurse more often than usual, eating once and then coming back for more feedings. It commonly happens during growth spurts or in the evening and can be stressful. Cluster feeding is a smart way for your baby to boost your milk supply, knowing feeding every hour or so is the best way to trigger your body to produce more" (O'Connor 2023). At the time, I didn't know what cluster feeding was, and considering my already fragile emotional state, it sent me into a sleep-deprived, anxiety-induced panic.

My daughter, who had been feeding every four hours in the hospital, was up every forty-five minutes on our first night home. My thoughts spiraled, "This can't be normal. She must be sick. Or maybe she's not getting enough milk, and I'm starving her. Does she have gas? Is she constipated? Is she in pain? Am I not holding her right?" What was I doing wrong that the nurses at the hospital had obviously done right? I had no control. She was in charge, and I was completely swimming blind in a sea of doubt. As the nights went on, things got a bit better, but my daughter was never what you'd call a "natural" sleeper. On a good night, she'd give me about two to three hours of shut-eye at a time, but she liked to eat, she liked to be held, and she liked to call the shots. Gary was always a trooper. He wordlessly got up when she woke, changed her diaper, and brought her to me. Though I envied his ability to fall right back to sleep, I appreciated we were a team.

At three weeks old, we noticed Mia's irritable time—early evening—started getting longer. One hour became two hours, and soon two hours became five or even six hours. She was growing… right into colic. Research and her pediatrician shared that colic is when "a baby who is healthy cries for more than three hours a day, more than three days a week. Colic spells happen at the same time of day, most often starting in the early evening, and often include high-pitched crying or screaming. A colicky baby is very hard to soothe, they can have a red face or pale skin around their mouth, and they may pull in their legs, stiffen their arms, arch their back, or clench their fists. Doctors aren't sure what causes colic but know it often starts when a baby is about 2–5 weeks old and gets better by the time the baby is 3–4 months old" (Karten 2019).

She cried from roughly five o'clock until ten or eleven o'clock at night—every night. Her cry was a high-pitched wailing with a scrunched-up, beet-red face. She would tense up her body and arch her back. We changed her, fed her, and swaddled her. I altered my diet, thinking it might be gas, but nothing stopped the nighttime crying. So, we walked. And we walked some more. We'd take turns doing laps around the hallways of our house. We'd sing, make up stories, bounce her, rock her, and pat her. I loved when Gary would pull up a chair close to the TV, put on a basketball game, and give our baby girl a detailed running commentary on whatever was happening on the screen. In the hours of insanity, it was a brief moment of comedy that made me laugh, appreciative for a husband who was present and supportive. If we were lucky, then she would stop crying. But it was usually only a momentary distraction before she'd gear up once again and resume her hysterics.

It was the dead of winter, so it was dark by five o'clock at night, which made the nights feel even more isolated and lonely. I dreaded her bewitching hours and was desperate for Gary to get home from work each day. On the nights when he came home late because of a work obligation or spending time with his oldest daughter, I went through the ineffective motions alone. And I was resentful, not for the lack of help but for the freedom he had to be anywhere but home. There were times when I laid her in her crib, shut the door, and cried. Sometimes, I just needed my arms free for a few minutes. As days turned into weeks, I developed a sense of numbness. I was still highly aware of her crying, but the panic and urgency eased because we recognized the pattern and realized we just had to wait it out. We had an odd feeling of control in knowing the ensuing chaos would, in fact, occur even though we had no control over it. It's a dichotomy for sure, but exactly the mindset necessary to tackle a roller coaster, and one we would need to tightly embrace while remaining steadfast and committed to parenting our daughter.

Motherhood can be completely foreign territory; it's like being dropped off in the middle of nowhere without a map or compass. It comes with comparison, self-doubt, and loneliness. If you don't have others to talk to or lean on, then the isolation can quickly lead to depression. I recently read, "American mothers often find people are more concerned about them before the birth of their baby, frequently asking how she's feeling, throwing showers, and required to attend regular prenatal checkups. After she has her baby, however, mother-focused support rapidly declines. Once home, her partner will probably return to work within the week, and she is left alone to make sure she has enough to eat, care for the house and new baby, teach herself to breastfeed, and heal from birth. Those who gave her attention during her pregnancy are no longer there, and the people who do come around are often more interested in the baby. She's not seen by a doctor until her six-week postpartum checkup, and if there are resources in her community that may help, she has no idea where they are and feels too overwhelmed to seek them out for herself. So, she must fend for herself as best she can" (Kendall-Tackett 2017).

I remember wanting to run to the store one day, but my baby liked to cry—loudly and often. She probably sensed my jacked-up nerves, and she refused the pacifier. My solution was, don't leave the house. It never crossed my mind to ask someone to watch her while I ran an errand. In hindsight, it wasn't a healthy decision. It led to feelings of isolation and loneliness, which is why I'm here encouraging others to do better. I didn't want to impose on anyone or come across as weak for needing help. And I was scared. I was nervous she would start to cry while we were out. God forbid people would hear her and deem me a bad mom because, other than nursing her, I didn't know how to soothe her yet. Ah, the insecurities I had being a new mama. Years later, with my second and third babies, errands were a necessity and my babies cried. Sometimes, there was blood-curdling, air-gasping, red-faced screaming as I quickly tried to bag up my groceries. Also, while my toddlers most likely ran wild and had tantrums over the candy that I refused to buy them. Guess what? No one called social services. I might've gotten a few looks, but no one died. I got more confident, and shit got done.

LOVE HARD TIPS
Managing the Baby Blues

1. "Know what to expect. While you're pregnant, talk to your mom or friends who have had children about their experiences after giving birth. Ask your doctor questions. Knowledge is power, and being prepared can help. Make a list of things that calm you down or make you happy, such as a hot bath or going for a walk. That way, when you're feeling overwhelmed or sad, you can refer to that list.
2. Get enough sleep. You can't stop your baby from waking up at all hours of the night, but you can limit caffeine, switch off your electronic devices an hour before bed,

and let your partner bottle feed once in a while so you can sleep through the night.

3. Get out of the house. Having a new baby can feel isolating. Meet up with friends for coffee. Talk to them about what you are feeling. Connect with other new moms. There can be strength in numbers. And don't forget to enjoy the fresh air; you'll find it may also help you sleep better!

4. Don't expect too much. You might feel tempted to compare yourself to the "perfect" moms you see on TV and social media. Don't give in to that pressure. Give yourself time to heal from childbirth and adjust to your new parenting role.

5. Ask for help. Tell your partner, family, or friends exactly what they can do for you. This could be taking care of your little one while you shower or go to the store or making a few meals so you can enjoy time with your newborn.

6. Up to 15 percent of new mothers experience postpartum depression, which is a debilitating condition that can take a toll on you and your family if not treated properly. Watch for extreme sadness and excessive crying, intense irritability or anger, severe anxiety, overwhelming fatigue or loss of energy, withdrawing from family and friends, or a reduced interest in activities you normally enjoy. Postpartum depression is a serious problem that should not be ignored. If you feel scared or out of control, tell your health care provider. If you're worried about hurting yourself or your baby, call 9-1-1" (Morgan 2020).

CHAPTER THREE

———

Don't tell a mother she looks tired; she already knows that. Tell her she's doing a good job; she may not know that.

—STEPHANIE PELTIER

Two things will wake a mother from her deepest sleep: (1) a child silently standing beside her bed. If they're breathing, she'll wake up, and (2) the smallest peep in the dead of night that could, in any way, be coming from one of her young. So now imagine the reaction a middle of the night, violent, blood-curdling shriek evokes. It's less "Hmm, I wonder what's wrong with my sweet girl" and more "Holy mother of God, who or what is torturing my child!"

Three years have gone by, and we've added a baby boy to our nest. Ty was the opposite of Mia in so many ways. I had no placenta previa and, therefore, no bedrest and a vaginal birth to her C-section. Ty had a head full of black hair to her peach fuzz and a laid-back, chill demeanor to her colic. Mia loved her new brother, and I was amazed at how easy a new baby could be. He required so much less than she had, which was a blessing as we ventured into another loop on the roller-coaster ride of Mia.

She started having nightmares. I'd abruptly wake up to her screams with my heart pounding and hairs on end, and I'd rush to her room to try and comfort her. But my touch and words only agitated her. She would get aggressive and angry. Sometimes, she'd storm about her room and try to open her windows. Other times, she'd move from bed to floor to closet and back, all while screaming incoherently or yelling, "Stop!" Her tirade would carry on until she would finally slowly start to settle down, crawl back into bed, and return to sleep.

Her nightmares concerned me. They were violent. Her heart rate would skyrocket, and she'd start to sweat. I had no idea what was happening to her or what I should do. I was afraid she might accidentally hurt herself by falling down the stairs, breaking a window, or running into something.

I tried tapping into Gary's parenting experience with his oldest daughter by frequently asking him, "Did you ever experience any of this with K when she was little?"

Gary replied, "I remember her having bad dreams but nothing like this. I could comfort her, and she'd go back to sleep."

Sometimes, Gary would come to Mia's room after an episode had been going on long enough to wake him too. He'd stand in the doorway and watch. But at times, he would try to hold her, which always sent her into a more aggressive fit.

I remember one night, I was desperate, alone, and out of ideas about what to do. I dug out our handheld camcorder and, while sitting in Mia's doorway in the dark, pressed record. I needed someone else to at least hear one of her episodes, tell me what was happening, and tell me how I could help her. The next morning, I decided our pediatrician was the person to start with.

"There's something happening at night with Mia. She's had nightmares, but these are on another level. I know when it's a nightmare. I can hold her and comfort her through them. I can get her to wake up from a bad dream. I can't do any of that now. These are something else. She says she doesn't remember having them the next morning, but how can she not be more tired the following day? I made this tape. Would you please listen to it because I don't know what else to do. I'm exhausted and worried about her." I pleaded my case while sitting in the brightly lit exam room, holding Mia on my lap.

A few days later, I got a phone call. "I listened to the tape. I think Mia is having night terrors," our pediatrician said. "There is nothing wrong with her, and she should eventually grow out of them. Avoid touching her or trying to wake her, but make sure she's safe. If there are stairs nearby her room, you may want to block them off. I'll have my nurse send you some literature, but unfortunately, there's not much you can do. We'll talk again about this at her next well-check, but call with any questions."

In the documents she mailed me, I learned that "night terrors affect almost 40 percent of children. However frightening, they aren't usually a cause for concern, and most children outgrow them" (Mayo Clinic Staff 2021). It's common for a child experiencing a night terror to "suddenly show signs of panic and fear while remaining asleep. They may scream, flail, or kick while also having a racing heart, rapid breathing, flushed skin, and sweating. Although they might open their eyes and appear to be afraid of someone or something in the room, they are typically not responsive if someone tries to wake or comfort them. They may even attempt to fight or escape. Most night terrors last about 10 minutes but could go on for 30 to 40 minutes. After the episode, children often fall back into a deep sleep and typically have no memory of the night terror the next morning. When your child has a night terror, it's natural to want to comfort or wake them, but that may actually make the episode last longer or become more aggressive" (Pacheco 2023).

Night terrors are the devil disguised as your precious child. If Mia's head could've spun around all exorcist-like, I'm pretty certain it would have. The night terrors went on to disrupt my sleep not just for months but years. They woke any other humans sharing my home, cabin, hotel room, or neighboring hotel rooms. After doing research, I became rigid with her bedtime schedule. I made sure she followed a winding-down routine and got to bed at a set time. We also avoided sugar and TV before bed—all to help minimize or maybe avoid an episode. Our efforts were often unsuccessful.

I learned to be silently present—to ensure Mia's safety—while avoiding interaction or touch. Occasionally, Gary would still try to offer his help. He would watch from the hallway until he couldn't help himself and go to comfort her.

"You can't touch her, Gary! I told you that. You'll just make it worse," I would say in a condescending and frustrated tone.

Tired and now offended, he'd respond with, "Fine, sorry I tried to help you. I don't know what to do. I'll just go back to bed, but I need to get some sleep."

These were not our best moments as we tried to navigate unknown and very rough waters. Night after night, the screams and thrashing would start, wake me from my sleep, and end whenever they had run their course—often twenty to thirty minutes later. Mia never remembered having them, nor was she more tired in the morning. I, on the other hand, was running on fumes.

"I need a break. I'm not sure how many more nights I can do this," I remember telling Gary with exhaustion one evening. I hated asking for help. Back then, I believed it was a sign of weakness, and if I was a good mom, I'd be able to handle it all. I also knew Gary needed to be up and functioning the next day for his job.

"Why don't you try and sleep in the basement tonight?" he offered. "Maybe you won't hear her. I'll get up with her tonight. She'll be okay, and you need some sleep." Sometimes, it worked, and other times, my mama ears would still detect an episode occurring two floors above. Either way, I knew I was struggling—cracking. I was feeling anger and resentment toward my child, knowing full well she had no control over our nights.

I was feeling more mom-guilt. I loved Mia but hated the night terrors, and the more exhausted I got, the finer the line that separated the two. I'd get mad at her. I never punished her or even said my feelings out loud, but I definitely felt resentment. *Why can't she just sleep through the night? Why are these night terrors still happening? Why is it always my job to sit with her? Will she ever be normal?* I hate that I put that stress on my relationship with her. The expectations were simply impossible. But regularly interrupted sleep, much less with the ferocity of night terrors, is tiring. To survive, I pushed down my own needs, ignoring and minimizing my feelings of overwhelm, frustration, and anger, which was not healthy. As moms, we're allowed to be human because we are human! We struggle. We'll have good days and bad. We feel the good and the bad. And we're still good moms!

My relationship with Gary was starting to show tiny hairline fractures too. I became highly aware of what I deemed an "imbalance" of our workload. Remember, I was tired and emotional. In my mind, he got to drive to and from an office in a quiet car. While at work, he socialized with friends, went out for lunch, or got in a workout. Some nights, he might have a client meeting, which meant cocktails and dinner. There was no asking if that would work with me. He had his time to do what he wanted. I, however, took care of the house, the yard, appointments, shopping, and meal prep, all while having two kids to take care of. I had to schedule anything extra and ask if I could go out to make sure he could cover it.

I had no free time or me time. Even going to the bathroom included a kid or two.

In all fairness, he was the breadwinner and provided very well for our family. I was extremely thankful and grateful to Gary for working hard. I admired the passion and dedication he had for his job and was proud of how truly talented he was. Plus, I grew up watching the same type of "imbalanced" relationship work for my own parents. I appreciated that his hard work afforded me the opportunity of staying home. I never had to miss a moment with the kids while being stuck in every one of them.

I knew I wanted to be a stay-at-home mom. Logically, I knew for that to happen, Gary had to put in his hours at work. But I started questioning the fairness, and that is a death sentence to any marriage. "Fairness in a relationship is about understanding and working toward the needs of the relationship, not just the needs of each person. Fairness is about the flexibility that is necessary to meet everyone's needs, including that of the relationship. To achieve fairness in your relationship, there are three perspectives that need to be considered: yours, your partner's, and your relationship's. A key component of relationship fairness is balance. It is about finding the sweet spot that balances your needs, your partner's needs, and your relationship's needs" (Ladipo 2013).

When you start keeping track and expecting regular equality of responsibilities, then you are no longer showing love to your spouse. You are no longer working toward the overall success of your relationship and family. I've learned, in different seasons of life, a relationship will often be imbalanced with regard to who's doing more or less, but it can still be a healthy and fulfilling one. And we do because we love.

Through the sleep-deprived nights, the growing strain on my marriage, and my need to do it all, I continued to try and show up as the mom and wife I wanted the world to see me as and the one I believed I needed to be. I did this to remain in control, and I needed to do it perfectly and happily. My value came from the opinions and accolades of others. Unlike the corporate world, where you receive reviews and praise for a job well done, being a stay-at-home mom left me in a kind of value purgatory. I was waiting for and needing validation, but I was unsure who it should come from and when. I had a successful husband and a stepdaughter who was smart and athletic. I had a super cute three-year-old and a new son. I had a beautiful home and a cabin on a lake. Essentially, I had it all. But remember this, especially in today's world of social media and highlight reels, what lies behind the happy smiles, the perfect homes, and the designer clothes can tell a very different story—a story with chapters titled "Self-Doubt," "Overwhelm," and "Marital Strain."

Mia did finally outgrow night terrors around the age of eight or nine, and our household was able to resume a more consistent sleep schedule. We survived, but my journey was lonely, draining, and isolating because I wouldn't let myself ask for help. Many of us are familiar with flying. "When you fly on an airplane, the flight attendant instructs you to 'put your oxygen mask on first, before helping others.' If you run out of oxygen yourself, you can't help anyone else with their own mask. Taking care of others can easily deplete the caregiver, and if you don't take care of yourself, you can experience burnout, health problems, anxiety, frustration, and more" (Schilder 2019).

At the risk of stereotyping but also out of experience, I think as women, we are programmed to believe asking for help or taking time for ourselves equals weakness or failure. If you can't handle everything on your own, then you are somehow not enough. I'm here to say you are enough, and you are worthy of self-care and support. It is not selfish. It's necessary so that we are better able to show up strong for those we love.

I don't say any of this lightly. I know firsthand how easy it is to lose yourself, whether it's in the first couple of years or over many years of loving and caring for everyone else. Mia's night terrors, I would come to realize, were just the beginning of a slow and steady, out-of-control spiral that would quickly threaten my marriage, my sanity, and our family unit.

LOVE HARD TIPS
How to Prioritize Yourself as a Busy Mom

1. "Schedule Time for Yourself Every Day. To prioritize yourself, you have to be intentional about it. This means putting time on your daily schedule for yourself. The best time to do this is when everyone else in your home is asleep, when the house is completely quiet. Waking up early may not be your thing; however, it may be your best option if you want to prioritize yourself. So, whether it's 5:30 a.m. or during your lunch break at work, make sure there's an intentional time for you.

2. Exercise and Eat Healthily. The one thing you can't afford to neglect is your health. Many times, we get so busy with other responsibilities that exercising gets put on the back burner. Make moving around for at least thirty minutes a part of your daily routine. This takes intentional planning, but it's worth it. You'll also want to make sure you're fueling your body with healthy food. Remember that we eat to live, so eat well! Show your body that you love and appreciate it.

3. Ask For and Accept Help. There's no such thing as superwoman and there's also no prize for doing everything alone. It's important to be okay with asking for and accepting help. If you're feeling overwhelmed and stressed, don't try to just push through it. If you need a break from your kids, ask your spouse or a trusted adult to watch them while you decompress. You'll be a better and healthier mom for not trying to carry the world on your shoulders.

4. Learn to Say No. Setting boundaries can be tough. A part of setting boundaries is learning to say no. And, to be clear, "No," is a complete sentence with no further explanation needed. It's okay not to volunteer for everything or go to every playdate or party. If it's going to stress you out or cause anxiety, just say no.

5. Take a Solo Staycation. Every mom deserves some time off. One way to do that is by going on a staycation. A staycation is just an overnight or weekend stay at a local hotel. So, although you're still in town, you get to rent your own room and do whatever you want for the day. Be sure to budget for this so you can stay somewhere nice and be pampered. Put your phone on do not disturb, and take some time for yourself.

6. Pick up a Hobby. Your life needs to be more than work and caring for your family. Having a hobby is an outlet you can enjoy. The key here is making sure your hobby remains something fun that you can do. Some hobbies to consider include crafting, dancing or cooking classes, painting, or picking up a sport.
7. Go on a Social Media Fast. Sometimes, silencing your surroundings can be one of the best things you do for yourself. One way to do that is by going on a fast. You can fast from social media so that you aren't distracted from everyone else's life and can focus on yourself" (Alexander 2022).

CHAPTER FOUR

———

I didn't choose this life. I didn't choose this horrible, horrible condition. But I get to choose how to live with it; I have to choose how to live with it.

—MARK MANSON

A few months into the new year, I remember Gary and I being at a standoff in our dining room. We were trying hard to keep our voices low as the kids were in the next room. His tone was stern and unapologetic as he drew a line in the sand of our marriage. "This is seriously insane. I can't keep doing this. All this fighting. All the accusations. Our marriage isn't going to make it if something doesn't change. If you don't stop creating problems that don't exist. If you don't trust me more, and stop yelling at me for not helping or not being there but at the same time not letting me! You're pushing me away, Deb!" His body language screamed frustration, standing stiff against the wall with his jaw clenched and eyes ablaze. There was a sense of urgency and decisiveness to his words. "I don't know what you want, but I don't want to be in a marriage where all we do is fight."

Mia was three years old, Ty was six months, and my world was starting to implode. The roller coaster of my life was threatening to derail. On top of the regular night terrors, I was adjusting to my new role of full-time, stay-at-home parent while watching Gary continue to thrive at the office we once shared; we both had jobs in advertising. I had gone part-time after Mia was born. I had planned to transition home full-time once baby number two joined us. The new position was no surprise, but my reaction to it was. I felt isolated and, truth be told, boring. It had been 100 percent my wish and choice to stay home with our kids, but I wasn't adjusting as smoothly as I thought I would. It wasn't easy. It wasn't glamorous. It wasn't even fun a lot of days. It was tantrums, crying, diapers, constant messes, toys everywhere, food and snot smeared on my clothes, and rarely a quiet moment to be had. I missed my work clothes. I missed grown-up conversations. I missed coworkers and clients who appreciated me. I missed being Deb.

I recently found an old email, from me to Gary, stuck in a notebook. He was traveling for work, and it was evident I was wrestling with some big emotions in his absence.

"Mia's tearing apart our bed. Ty's chomping on his hands, desperate to eat again. And I'm missing you. And missing me. The old me. The fun me. The young me. The dressed-up me. The goofy me. The spontaneous me. The me that would finish a bottle of wine with you over venison, have great sex, then fall asleep in your arms. Sometimes I don't know where she is. Afraid that she's permanently gone. It makes me sad. Ha, here I am crying as I write this. Mia's crying over something

now, so I'll wrap this up. I really miss you. And you are
a good husband. Wouldn't trade you or even this time
with our kids for anything. I just want—no, need—help
sometimes. I feel alone and tired. Be safe. Come home
soon. I love you so much. Yours always, Deb."

Gary responded later that night.

"Thanks for the note. I know it's hard for you being
home with the kids all day. I couldn't do it, and I don't
know how you keep it together sometimes. You are a
very good mom and a good wife, and I always know
it will get better. I will miss you while I'm gone. And I
will think about you and the kids every day. Maybe we
can have venison Thursday night when I get back. I'll
see you then. Love always, Gar."

I was dealing with exhaustion, an unfamiliar new role, loss of
identity, and loneliness. But wait! Let's add more stress to my
mixed bag of emotions. At the same time, I was getting more
and more obsessive about my kids getting sick, more specifically, throwing up. This was no new fear of mine. Sometime
in middle school, I developed a deathly, all-consuming fear
of vomiting. I had panic attacks if I got a stomachache, or I
found out someone in my class had gotten the stomach flu.
My frantic pacing and incessant pleading for reassurance
would completely overwhelm and frustrate my mom, who
had no idea what my problem was and, therefore, had no way
of knowing how to help me. Her mind was dealing with logic,
while mine was not. I would often avoid or leave a situation
if someone threw up or felt like they were going to. I'd then
obsessively worry about if or when I was going to throw up.

I wouldn't feel "out of the woods" until five days had gone by, seemingly the appropriate incubation time in my mind. I hated throwing up even more than roller coasters.

Now, at home with little to do but focus on my kids, I became overwhelmed with trying to keep them from getting the stomach flu while still allowing them to be kids. The less control I felt over that—let's be real, kids are walking storm clouds of germs—the more I'd look for it in other areas of my life. Gary began to have less and less say over the house and kids and really couldn't do much right in my eyes. I reloaded the dishwasher when he did it "wrong." I'd get angry when he didn't help pick up the house. It wasn't because he refused to, just that his time frame was different than mine. I redecorated and rearranged room after room, temporarily reveling in the sense of control and cleanliness it provided me. And when Gary didn't "get" my stress about the kids throwing up, I'd get mad at him for not understanding when even I didn't understand why I was the way I was.

I was frustrated with myself and with him. I was filled with puke anxiety every day, and soon, my jealousy over Gary's work "freedom" morphed into insecure anger. I started picking fights and questioning his faithfulness. I blamed him for not helping me around the house or with the kids when it was really me standing in the way of what I wanted. I was so tired of worrying all the time and fighting my own insecurities. My shame was crushing and isolating. Failure and embarrassment were knots in my gut that cut off all air. I felt unworthy of all I was blessed with but couldn't appreciate.

That dining room argument was a pivotal moment in our five-year marriage. Like a spotlight, Gary had illuminated all my fears and worries and the unhealthy habits I had created to try and manage them. It was harsh and terrifying, and I felt ashamed. But at the same time, someone had finally called me out, and, in a way, it released me from struggling alone. I knew I needed help. I not only knew it, but I desperately wanted it. In that moment, my fight became ours. The elephant in the room had been exposed, and like anything that's brought from the dark shadows into the light, its power began to diminish. And so, I chose to find help. I chose us.

I recently asked Gary what he remembered about that time in our relationship. He reflected back, "I remember you were always paranoid about the kids getting sick. It's why we didn't go bowling. There were no playlands or church cry rooms. I also remember being tired of you always worrying about things that 'might' happen. It wrecked moments and situations. You worried so much that you missed out on fun. We didn't know at the time, obviously, that you were dealing with OCD, and I know I was really intolerant back then. I dealt with people who created problems at work all day at my job. I didn't want to do it when I got home. I know I was really impatient."

I started my search for a therapist by reaching out to both my primary care physician and my OB-GYN for recommendations. After phone calls, paperwork, and coordinating schedules, I had my first appointment on the calendar. I still get emotional remembering that very first meeting. Her office was soothing, her voice welcoming and warm. "It's really nice to meet you, Deb. Tell me a little bit about yourself and why you're here," she began. I was finally allowed and expected to share all the things I had kept hidden for so many years. Habits and struggles that left me confused and feeling ugly and broken. She changed my life. In our very first session, it was this wonderful woman who said, "You're not crazy, Deb. You have obsessive-compulsive disorder (OCD). It's treatable, and I can help you."

I learned, "OCD is a common condition. It causes persistent disturbing thoughts and compulsive rituals that attempt to ease a person's anxiety. OCD is diagnosed when rituals become consuming and interrupt daily life. While someone may know that their thoughts are unreasonable and not due to real-life problems, it's not enough to make the unwanted thoughts go away. Thankfully, medicines and therapy can help, and treatment is most successful when both are used together" (Johns Hopkins Medicine 2023).

When I hear someone refer to a mental health diagnosis as negative, for example, they won't seek help because they don't want to be labeled nor do they want their child "labeled," the hairs on the back of my neck stand up. I realize there are uneducated and insensitive people in the world. And from those people, a label can come with negative connotations. Someone diagnosed with mental illness, when not empowered or treated, might feel demeaned, defined, or confined by stereotypes and assumptions. But for me, that diagnosis— that "label"—was freedom. It was freedom from the ball-and-chain of shame, freedom from the ugliness of self-blame and self-hatred, and it released me from the constant need to question my mental stability. It identified a cause so we could manage the symptoms.

I could relate to a *New York Times* essay written by a man also diagnosed with OCD. He shared, "The [OCD] label was helpful. I went from drowning in a bottomless and unexplainable sea of terror to 'having OCD.' The label helped me make sense of my reality, pointed the way to a specific type of treatment, and made me feel less alone" (Stulberg 2022). The minute my therapist told me it wasn't my fault, I realized I wasn't broken or bad. She lifted a weight I'd been carrying around, an embarrassment, for over seventeen years. She explained, "Obsessive-compulsive disorder involves problems in communication between the front part of the brain and deeper structures of the brain that use a neurotransmitter"—basically, a chemical messenger—"called serotonin. In some people, the brain circuits involved in OCD become more normal with either medications called serotonin reuptake inhibitors (SRIs), cognitive behavior therapy (CBT), or both" (International OCD Foundation 2023).

I continued seeing my therapist frequently. She allowed me the opportunity to talk through my fears, taught me techniques and tools that would help me manage my obsessions, and offered to connect me with a psychiatrist so I could explore medication options if interested. I was filled with optimism for the first time in months, maybe even years. I was hopeful for me, my marriage, and finally for my parenting going forward. After years of living with what I thought was a broken brain, someone had the glue I needed to piece it back together.

LOVE HARD TIPS
Strategies to Manage Obsessive-Compulsive Disorder or
Anxiety

1. Deep Breathing Exercises. "Breathwork exercises are
   exceptionally helpful for managing anxiety related to
   OCD. There are many different types, but they all serve
   the purpose of slowing down the breath and heart rate,
   creating a calming effect" (Deupree 2023).
2. "Using the 4 Rs: Relabeling, Reattributing, Refocusing,
   and Revaluing.
   a. Relabel: Start by labeling what you're dealing with.
   b. Reattribute: Once you've identified what you're feeling,
      it's time to reattribute. Your brain may be screaming
      that what you're experiencing is because you're under-
      prepared, weak, or even unlovable. But in reality? It's
      your anxiety.
   c. Refocus: Now that you've gotten a handle on what
      you're experiencing and why, it's time to refocus your
      mind. Switch to another activity like doing a quick
      meditation, going for a walk around the block and
      listening to a podcast, or even journaling about what
      you're going through.
   d. Revalue: After relabeling, reattributing, and refocus-
      ing, it's time to revalue. Now that you've gained a little
      perspective, ask yourself:
      ▪ How accurate were my thoughts and urges?
      ▪ What would have happened if I gave into them?
      ▪ What would I like to do now?" (Shea 2021)
3. "Consider speaking with a mental health professional.
4. Try exposure response prevention (ERP). This type
   of therapy helps you manage obsessive thoughts and

compulsions by exposing you to the first ones and preventing you from engaging in the latter.

5. Try to develop effective distractions. Learning to quickly shift your attention away from intrusive thoughts may offer you some relief. Some ideas include washing your face with cold water, listening to loud music and dancing, focusing on deep breathing, and other relaxation techniques.

6. Consider exercising regularly. Exercise may help you reduce compulsions and elevate your mood. You may want to do some type of physical activity every day as a preventive habit" (Wright 2022).

CHAPTER FIVE

———

Pain is the invitation for God to move in and replace our faltering strength with His. We must invite God into our pain to help us survive.

—LISA TERKEURST

Like a roller coaster, life can have moments that are steady. When the ride is smooth, those you love are healthy, your job is fulfilling, and you are comfortable.

Then all of sudden, life can throw you a curveball—an unexpected death, the loss of a job, divorce—and the ride gets jerky and rough. Your world shatters and the best you can do is ride out the emotional free fall. You might question the goodness and love of a God who promises deliverance and hope. You wonder how you can trust Him when you don't understand what's happened. I soon found myself at the foot of Jesus, begging Him to help me find my footing and the will to move forward.

Two months had gone by since the relief of my diagnosis, and as I stood with my family in a pew at church, I suddenly felt this whoosh-like wave of light-headedness followed quickly by nausea. I didn't feel right. To avoid a scene, I left the sanctuary. I hustled to the car where, hunched over in the front seat, I broke out in a cold sweat. I was either going to faint or throw up. When the panic started to set in, I worked to use the tools my therapist was teaching me. I focused on deep breathing and thought through why this might be happening. Did I eat something bad? Was I overtired? Maybe I was coming down with something? Had I been around someone sick? Slowly, the nausea subsided, leaving me weak but no longer faint, and I was able to sit upright.

A few weeks later, I missed my period. It dawned on me when the last time was that I nearly passed out in public. I drove to the nearest drug store and bought myself a three-pack of pregnancy tests. Oh, did I pass them with flying colors—pregnant, pregnant, and yep, still definitely pregnant. "Umm, nope. This was not in my plan, Lord! Not now! Not yet," I remember telling God. Mia was still three and Ty was only eight months. Gary and I had worked hard to conceive each of them—planning, temperature taking, timing. It took over a year of "practice" to finally win their conception games. This baby, on the other hand, was a complete surprise. I would need time to wrap my head around our news.

At my next therapy appointment, I shared our news with my psychologist.

"You should know that, though it's still early, I found out last week that I'm pregnant. Gary and I weren't trying, so this is a huge shock!"

"How are you feeling about it, Deb?" she asked.

"I'm not sure yet. I mean, I love being a mom, and I know this baby is a gift, but it's so soon after Ty. He won't even be two when I have this baby, and I'm already overwhelmed. And I'm just starting to get a better handle on my OCD and feeling really excited about working with you on getting better. I'm scared," I told her honestly.

"What about Gary? How is he taking it?" she asked.

"He's good. Really happy actually. He leaves for elk hunting next week, so I wanted to tell him before he left."

"Well, we will still work on managing your anxiety, and we'll still schedule regular meetings throughout your pregnancy. Let's take it week-by-week and see how things go," she reassured me. "As far as medication, my recommendation would be to hold off on starting anything. There are many we can try, and 'most antidepressants, especially the selective serotonin reuptake inhibitors (SSRIs) often used to treat OCD, are generally considered safe throughout pregnancy' (Marks 2022). However, I'd prefer to have you hold off on the trial and error that goes along with finding the right one until after you deliver. If your symptoms become unmanageable, we can always revisit the idea further into your pregnancy," she advised.

It was the oddest mix of emotions. I was giddy, finally having a surprise pregnancy! A baby that was truly God's plan for us and not ours. On the other hand, I was panicky about having to hold off on the mental freedom I had been very hopeful about. My thoughts swirled with all the ways things would be more difficult. We moms have to make choices and start compromising right from conception. This was no different. I loved this baby the minute I saw two pink lines and didn't want to do anything that could potentially put them at risk. And on a positive note, the news of this unexpected blessing along with my recent diagnosis brought Gary and me closer. I was hopeful and excited as was he. I continued with my therapy sessions. Gary had a new appreciation for my struggles and was supportive, more understanding, and patient. Our focus became our marriage and preparing to have three kids under four in less than nine months. I was working to control the things I could control and finally learning how to accept or let go of the things I couldn't.

Weeks went by quickly with the busyness that was two littles. At eight weeks, I started prenatal checkups. Based on my last period, they estimated I was due the following May, and they ran the standard blood and urine tests. All results came back normal. At twelve weeks, the baby's heartbeat was strong and steady, and I was measuring on track and healthy. We got through the first trimester, told our families, the kids, and started telling friends and extended family. It was a relief to finally share our big surprise. My body was changing and growing much more quickly having done pregnancy twice before, and it had gotten harder to hide my growing abdomen. At sixteen weeks, I had another wellness check. Gary had a meeting, and I had no problem going solo as I knew the drill by now. My nurse came into the exam room, made some small talk, asked all the standard questions, had me lay back, and lubed up my belly for a heartbeat check.

The absence of a heartbeat when one is meant to be there is *deafening*.

Five seconds go by.

Then seven.

Then longer.

She was trying to reassure me while manipulating the fetal Doppler wand—"the handheld device used to check a baby's heartbeat" (Valeii 2021)—up, down, and all around. She was pressing more firmly into my abdomen.

"Hmm, baby's being stubborn," the nurse said with a forced lightness. "You're still fairly early in your pregnancy, so sometimes it takes a little longer. Baby could be sitting lower today."

Cue the nerves. I might've even inappropriately giggled because that's what I do when I'm frightened or anxious. I went into that checkup feeling confident and presumptuous. New life is a miracle, and I had undervalued how precious and fragile it could be. After a few more unproductive swirls, she wiped off my belly, lowered my shirt, and asked me to follow her.

She ushered me to the ultrasound room, where a technician was waiting. No more small talk. The unease and seriousness of the situation was stifling. The lights went out, gel was reapplied to my belly, and we both watched as the glow of the ultrasound screen filled the room. What had always been a beautiful experience watching my baby float like a lima bean, their little heart a pulsing blip on the screen, was now heartbreaking as I stared at a picture of my baby completely quiet and still. No flips and turns. No moving limbs. No blips. I remember hearing a nurse, or maybe it was the ultrasound tech, talking, but it sounded like the teacher in Charlie Brown cartoons. Muffled, garbled, and far away, as though my ears were protecting my heart from this devastating news. They cleaned up my stomach and helped me off the table. I zipped up my pants and pulled down my shirt. I had started crying.

"I'm so sorry Deborah. You can leave through this back door to avoid the waiting room. Someone will call you later today to schedule your induction at the hospital," I heard the nurse say.

I realized why they ushered me out inconspicuously. I was sobbing. I didn't want to deal with others seeing me, nor did happy, expectant mamas need the reminder that bad, unexpected things could happen behind those closed doors. But, in that moment, all alone, I felt like such a mom-failure. Sneaking out the back in shame because my body had betrayed me and my baby.

When I got to the car, alone and still shocked by how much my life had changed in just one hour, I called Gary's office. I needed him so badly.

"Hi June, I'm calling for Gary," I fought to speak coherently when my friend and company receptionist answered.

"I'm sorry, Deb. He's still meeting with clients. Can I give him a message?"

"No, please get him. It's an emergency," I pleaded.

"Hi. What's up?" Gary asked worriedly and a little out of breath minutes later. I was envious of the naivety he still had, even though I could hear the concern over what could possibly be important enough to have him pulled from his meeting.

"I lost the baby. It died," I cried.

"What! Where are you? Are you still at the doctor's office?" he asked, shocked.

"I'm in the parking lot. I have to call my mom and tell her. I have to pick up the kids from her house. What will I say?"

"I'll come get you. I don't think you should drive anywhere. Shit, I'm so sorry, hon," Gary was doing his best to stay calm until he could be with me.

"I can get to my mom's house. She's only ten minutes away. I don't want to sit here alone in this parking lot. I'll wait there for you," I said.

"I'm leaving now. I love you," he said, and we hung up.

I called my mom next. Blubbering through a quick update of what happened and promising to drive safely. When I got to my childhood home, my parents' house, she met me in the driveway with tears in her eyes. I sank into her and grieved for the life I would no longer have with my baby.

Ty was too young, but at almost four, Mia knew about her new baby brother or sister and had been excited. It tore me apart to try and explain to her that I was okay despite the fact that something had happened to our baby. I told her the baby was sick and needed to get checked. I wasn't ready to tell her sweet face that it had died. I knew she would worry while I was in the hospital and tried to reassure her. "Mommy is okay but has to go to the hospital so the doctors can see what's wrong with our baby. I'll be there for a couple of days and come home as soon as I can. You can call me whenever you're scared or nervous."

My mom came over to our house later that night. She would stay with the kids for the time we needed to be at the hospital. After we all went to bed, I remember quietly walking to the room my mom was staying in, and for the first time since I was a child, crawling under the covers and nestling in close to her. Needing the love and support from my own mom as I prepared to say goodbye to my child. I remember her whispering, "I wish I could take this pain from you. I wish I could suffer instead," as she stroked my hair. My pain was deep and searing and overwhelming but somehow bearable in that moment while protected in the love and comfort of her arms.

I was admitted to the hospital the following day to begin the induction process because "it is typically not safe for a woman to wait for the pregnancy to deliver on its own with a second-trimester loss as there is a high chance of having significant bleeding. Medicine is placed directly on the cervix to cause dilation and hopefully induce labor within one to two days" (Santiago-Munoz 2018). The level of care and respect the staff showed me was incredible. I was given a private room down from the "active" labor and delivery rooms, protecting me from the cries of healthy new babies and joyful mamas. The nurses were kind, empathetic, and accommodating. A chaplain came to visit. I was given a memory box containing a hospital band and a tiny hospital hat to represent and remember our baby. They offered us the option to have the remains of our baby buried with others also lost early, in a group gravesite, at a nearby cemetery.

One of the first things I did when I got set up in my hospital room was request another ultrasound. I had to for my own peace of mind. What if they were wrong? What if my baby came back to life or had just been sleeping? I could feel the mound of my abdomen reminding me that my child was still physically there. I needed to check once more before starting the process to remove them from my womb. They may have rolled their eyes, knowing medically that ultrasounds don't lie, but they were kind and respectful regardless. They acquiesced and soon an ultrasound tech joined us, wheeling his portable machine. Gary and I sat glued to the monitor as our baby's image appeared, the picture confirming our loss—no heartbeat, no movement, no life. It was the first and last time Gary would see our baby. When they left, he sagged onto the bed beside me. His world shattered too. "I'm so glad I saw our baby. You have them inside you. They're part of you, so of course, you feel this loss deeply. But now, after getting to see him or her, it made this very real for me too. I'm so sorry, Deb. I'm so sorry," he sobbed as we held each other.

Gary fielded calls from our friends and family and stayed by my side the entire time. He held me close through waves of the most intense grief I had ever experienced, my body shaking with heartbreak. He sat back when I became irritable and upset both from the situation and the meds, and he offered light banter to help distract me and pass time. Mia struggled with my absence, and we decided to have her come for a quick visit on day two. When she walked through the door and rushed up and into bed beside me, my world was temporarily righted. Her smile, hugs, kisses, and touch were all incredibly healing. She was curious about the room, the bathroom, the fun controls for the TV, and my bed. We snuggled and talked. I was finally able to tell her that our baby had died and was playing in heaven with Jesus. She asked why, to which I had no answer other than honesty, "I don't know, Mia. Jesus wasn't ready to give him or her to us just yet. Just know that mommy is not hurt or sick, and I can't wait to come back home to you."

Though there was some initial pain and spotting, nothing more happened physically. After three long and emotional days of waiting, medicating, and grieving, my body refused to deliver and instead developed a fever. The decision was made to schedule a surgical evacuation or dilation and curettage (D&C), which is a procedure where "your ob-gyn passes a small tool through the cervix and into the uterus to remove the tissue in an operating room and using general anesthesia" (Cohen 2022).

There would be a lot of hurting and healing once I left the hospital and in the days and months to come. My stomach remained distended for weeks. Where it had been firm, it was now soft and empty. My milk came in, another painful reminder of my lost baby. And I continued to battle guilt over the miscarriage. I obsessed over what I may or may not have done to cause it even though every nurse and doctor had reassured me it wasn't my fault. The genetic testing came back negative for any chromosomal abnormalities and also determined that we were having a boy. It was a bittersweet phone call to get. There wasn't a logical reason why the miscarriage happened, and for me, that was a challenging verdict to live with.

As time went by, life around me seemed to return to normal while I continued to struggle. Guilt followed me like a shadow—for drinking the glass of wine I had previously given up, for laughing or moments of joy, for anything pleasurable or carefree, for slowly moving forward. I also continued to struggle with the *why*. Why did God gift me an unplanned baby just to take it back? I was short with Gary, and as much as I asked for his support, I did a good job of pushing him away. I wanted him to be stuck in grief with me, and because he wasn't, or dealt with his grief differently, I was resentful and annoyed.

I also wanted to talk about our loss and discuss the idea of maybe trying again one day, but when he didn't say what I wanted to hear, I stormed off angry.

"I know it's only been a few weeks, and I'm not sure I'll ever be ready again, but do you have any thoughts or feelings about trying again for another baby down the road?" I asked him one night as we sat by the fire.

"I don't think we should, Deb. I'm getting older, and I don't want you to go through that again. I feel like I'm done," he said definitively.

"How can you say that? How can you not even consider the possibility? What if I'm not done?"

Even though he had every right to his feelings, and I had asked him to share them with me, I wasn't ready for the door to be permanently closed.

I was grateful to have a therapist already in place who I could work with to process and get through that loss. Gary joined me once so we could talk through our post-miscarriage emotional conflict and find resolution. I continued to work on my OCD, and in time, I decided to start medication. The first drug we tried was Lexapro, and pretty early on, I noticed subtle improvements. Slowly recognizing that I no longer felt the need to reload the dishwasher and worrying a little less when a child in my kid's class got the stomach flu. It took a few months to determine my optimal dosage, and during that time, I continued seeing my therapist. I finally started feeling like the me I had hoped and dreamed of being.

We miscarried in November 2003. I worked hard on myself and my grief through the winter. We recognized what would have been our baby's due date May 5, 2004. Then, after many prayers and lengthy discussions, we decided to try once more for another child in September of that same year. God knew my mama heart was scared and still bruised, which is why I believe He gifted me with our sweet Zoe the very first month we worked to conceive. I will always mourn the "what ifs" and "could've beens" of losing my boy, but I simply cannot imagine life without our amazing baby girl. She was our rainbow after the storm.

Through my miscarriage, there was growth. I leaned into my relationship with Jesus, desperately needing His strength to hold me up. I prayed and talked with Him often. In the days following my miscarriage, I was mad. I remember sitting outside on a cold November night, staring up into the starry night sky with tears streaming down my face and fists clenched, yelling, "*Why*? I'm so angry at you! I know I'm not supposed to doubt you, but I do. I feel lost. You allowed me to be hurt, and I don't understand!" The icy air and heavy darkness was a perfect backdrop for the blackness I felt.

With time though, my heart began to heal and soften. Gary and I gave our son a name and with it, an identity. I visited the site where he had been buried. I talked about him with our kids, close friends, and family. Gary gifted me with an ornament for our Christmas tree. I found the most healing knowing our son would be remembered. I started talking to God as though we were coparents. Sharing things I wanted my son to know.

"How's my baby boy up there? Tell him I can't wait to meet him. His sister and brother would give him a run for his money. It would bring me such joy to watch them play together! Does he have blond or brown hair? What about his eye color? Athlete or artist? Man, I can't wait to hear his laugh," I'd chatter on.

Some discussions were casual and some were hard.

"I'm really struggling today. I miss him. There's this emptiness. I don't understand. I'm trying. I'm trusting. Please hold me up and show me your path."

It gave me a sense of peace knowing I didn't have to shoulder the pain alone.

And some talks were with my boy. "I saw Maddie yesterday. You and she had due dates in the same week. She's crawling! It made me wonder what you would be doing. I miss you so much. It's always bittersweet to see her—alive and healthy. And yet, it helps me stay connected to you. I see you through her. I love you," I'd remind my baby. I talk to him still to this day. The mystery of who he would be now at nineteen is incomprehensible.

Good came from our loss. My faith grew stronger when I had to let go and let God in. When I struggled with control, He took it from me so I could learn to survive without it. It also introduced me to an amazing community of women who encircled me with support and love, having miscarried at some point themselves. They knew my pain. They knew the emptiness. They didn't try to make it better. Instead, they sat in the suck with me and held my hand when I felt strong enough to navigate through it. They also knew healing and hope. Friends, strangers, and acquaintances brought me meals, said prayers for me, and sent me cards of encouragement.

God allowed me a few months with my child before needing him back, and I was grateful. Grateful to have been his mom, even for a short time. God orchestrated his conception and allowed his death. Even though I could not comprehend His wisdom in those decisions, I was comforted in my belief that there was a better, brighter, happier life after this earthly one. I chose to focus on the excitement of one day being together again.

I hate that a miscarriage community exists, but I am very grateful to have had it. To all the women who stepped up when I needed it and shared their own stories of surviving loss, you were truly put in my life by a God who knew I would need you.

And to those struggling right now, it's a roller coaster. The journey is difficult, but remember that you are not alone.

LOVE HARD TIPS
How to Cope after Miscarriage

1. "Give your body and mind time to heal. Time is often the best healer. Your body needs time to get back to normal, and so does your mind and emotional health.
2. Let yourself grieve the loss. Allow yourself to go through the grieving process, from shock, anger, guilt, and depression to acceptance. If you feel like you need to cry, then cry. Stop to acknowledge your loss. If your feelings of sadness are long-lasting, talk with your doctor.
3. Get support. When you're ready, share your feelings with your partner, family, and friends. Join a web-based forum with other women who have gone through pregnancy loss. Talk to a religious or spiritual leader, a counselor, or therapist.

4. Commemorate your baby. It can be tough to move on emotionally without some sort of closure. Have a small ceremony to say goodbye, make a memory box, write a farewell letter, commemorate your child's life in a special garden, get a special piece of jewelry with a birthstone—whatever feels right for you" (Jensen 2020).

5. "Expect misguided comments, even from good friends. Try to remind yourself that people don't mean to be hurtful. They probably feel helpless and awkward, so they blurt out the first thing they think of.

6. You'll want a spokesperson. To avoid repeating your sad news over and over again—and sitting through botched attempts at sympathy—enlist the help of a sensitive friend or family member" (Moore 2017).

CHAPTER SIX

—

Living with anxiety is like being followed by a voice. It knows all your insecurities and uses them against you. It gets to the point when it's the loudest voice in the room. It's the only one you can hear.

—UNKNOWN

"No! I don't want to go to school! You can't make me!" Mia shouted at breakfast, repeatedly kicking the stool she was on. "My tummy hurts! I'm *not* going to school!"

And here we go.

"Mia, you're not sick. You were fine just a little bit ago. You have to go to school," I'd firmly and confidently reassure her.

"But, my tummy really, really hurts!"

I'll admit, initially, I thought she was being dramatic to get attention. Then, after time, I thought she was being manipulative. I thought she was trying to get away with staying home by making excuses about her stomach hurting. But eventually, I realized there was something much bigger in control. Something that dominated her thoughts and feelings, and eventually culminated in angry outbursts.

At the start of first grade, my previously social and independent daughter developed separation anxiety. Remember that roller coaster I talked about? Isn't it so true, moms—especially of littles—that when you finally seem to get into a rhythm, find your groove, and get a little comfortable, wham, illness or travel or a new phase pops up, and all normalcy to date spirals into obscurity? At school drop-off, Mia would protest, cling to me, and cry until the teacher—bless her soul—would gently take her by the shoulders and steer her into the classroom. "Come on Mia, let's go into the classroom. Come help me feed the bunny," she would say, attempting to distract and disentangle her from my waist. It broke my heart to leave her so distraught, but this had not been normal behavior in the past, so I chalked it up to a temporary glitch in our relationship that we'd work through. But rather than improve as I anticipated, mornings got more difficult. Mia became overwhelmed with seemingly small tasks like getting dressed, eating breakfast, and brushing her hair. She would fly off the handle in fits of irrational rage yelling, hitting, and calling names.

Thursday, November 16, 2006

"Excellent morning! Sticker for surprising me, all dressed before I was even awake. So happy! No tummy ache or headache in the morning. Forty-five minutes into the morning, her mood changed. Her hair was frustrating her—in her face, yelling at me to "fix it"—and angry

that shoes were hard to get on. They weren't untied. Started stomping and yelling. Then yelled at me that I wasn't being happy. Sad and cranky when leaving for school—what happened? Happy in the truck with dad on the way to school. Headache at bedtime."

Friday, November 17, 2006

"Picked her outfit—one of her favorites. It was clean, which made for a happy morning until we had to brush hair. Yelling at me to do it, yelling that I was using the wrong spray, yelling at me NOT to brush it. Unhappy at breakfast. Don't know why. Okay, in the car—I took her—and at school."

Saturday, November 18, 2006

"Woke up happy and on her own—no school so no pressure. Had trouble making a decision at Build-a-Bear, which caused a tummy ache. Said her tummy felt sick. Went away when we got home and she no longer felt pressure to pick a toy. Tummy and headaches at bedtime."

Wednesday, November 29, 2006

"Good Morning! Dressed first. Happy girl. No tummy aches. Lots of sticker rewards!"

Thursday, November 30, 2006

"Not such a good morning. Cranky and yelling right from the start. Woke up on her own but angry and yelling that the lights were too bright. Angry about her hair. Angry that I can't take her to school. Lots of yelling, stomping, and hitting. Got a time-out for not choosing better words after our one-two-three countdown warning. Dad finally had to pick her up and carry her to the truck for school."

Journal entries helped me identify a developing pattern. It was clear that decision-making caused Mia stress, which triggered angry outbursts. I started to work with her on planning outfits the night before, choosing her lunch items before bed so there was less to discuss and decide come morning, and rewarding her with stickers for positive behavior. My hope was to manage or eliminate the pressure of indecision and therefore avoid conflict. But no matter what attempt was made, there still seemed to be tasks that set her off and overwhelmed her to the point of breaking.

Two months into the year, I started getting calls from the school office during the day saying Mia wasn't feeling well and was asking to come home. "Hi Mom. My tummy hurts. Can I come home?" she'd ask, her voice shaking.

The first couple of times, I did bring her home, and soon she was laughing and playing perfectly fine. After that, when she would call, I would start with, "I'm sorry you don't feel good, but I think you're okay. Remember last time how you came home, but then you were fine? I want you to go back to class, and if you still don't feel good later, you can call me again." If she'd persist, I'd try and distract her with conversation, "Did you go outside for recess? How was lunch? When you get home from school, what should we play?"

Eventually, our bedtime routine was affected by her anxiety too. More and more frequently, my daughter would tell me her stomach hurt during nighttime prayers and kisses. I assumed she was just stalling until she started asking the question, "Am I going to throw up?" Little did I know, way back in the first grade, that one question would become the mantra of our relationship.

It was my lightbulb moment. My "A-ha, I see exactly what's going on now" realization. Because "Am I going to throw up?" had been my question. Let's go back in time to the eighties. I ran track in high school. I joined the team to be with friends and because it was a no-cut sport. Surprisingly, I turned out to be slightly above average at it, earning ribbons, medals, and state qualifications. As is the case for a lot of competitors, my stomach would hurt before races. Logically, we know nerves are not only normal but healthy. But remember, I had a very illogical fear of throwing up that no one knew about. I was blessed to find a lifeline in one of my coaches. She quickly filled the role of "track mom" for me, and the more comfortable I became with her, the more I looked to her for constant reassurance. Four years of a ritual was born, and it grew into my compulsion.

Some people with OCD might flip a light switch on and off or wash their hands compulsively. For me, it was repeating a pattern. At a meet, for the first call of my running event over the loudspeaker, I'd begin to search for my coach. Once I found her, I'd ask her two questions, "Am I going to do okay?" and "Will I throw up?"

She'd calmly take me by both arms, look me in the eyes, smile, and reassure me with, "No, Debbie. You are not going to throw up. You are going to be fine. Now go run your race." She might've thought it was a bit odd, but I also think she loved me enough to play the game—ritual completed, reassurance received. I'd then find my team and continue to warm-up for my event. I did this at every single race.

Living with a fear of throwing up, which I've recently learned is clinically called emetophobia, is isolating, lonely, and shameful. If you're young, you're scared. As you grow older and recognize the irrationality of your thoughts, you're still scared, but you also feel like a crazy person. It's embarrassing because the majority of the world, and most often your peer group, doesn't worry to the extreme that you do. Oh sure, if you say something like, "Oh, I hate throwing up" around friends, they'll nine times out of ten reply back with a "Oh, me too. So disgusting." But while you're still in your head, obsessing and anxious, they've moved on in the conversation to what tomorrow's assignment is or when the football game starts.

You battle your mind as it spirals round and round—completely stuck on a hamster wheel—knowing the anxiety you're feeling is ridiculous but not at all being able to reign it in or control it. While everyone else is moving forward, you remain rooted in self-talk and obsession. On a successful day, you're able to "tough it out." Sometimes though, it gets bad enough that you pace, experience chest pain, feel a shortness of breath, and finally need to remove yourself from a situation before you expose yourself. Once in a safe place, you work to regain control and calm. Over the years, I was also able to find a couple of lifelines who played a role similar to my high school track coach. A close friend and, eventually, my mom would reassure me at the height of a panic attack. They would tell me, "You will not throw up." It didn't matter if I ever did. I just needed to hear those five words. As explained in a blog found on the Healthline website, "People with emetophobia are usually aware that their reaction to the object of their phobia isn't typical, but this knowledge generally isn't helpful and often just makes the experience more distressing. It can also lead to feelings of shame, causing them to hide their symptoms from others" (Saripalli 2023).

Being a mom who has an extreme fear of vomiting is very complicated and often physically and mentally debilitating. Newborns spit up—some more than others. Babies and toddlers puke—all over everything. Ty, as a baby, had a sensitive gag reflex. It was so triggering to me that I didn't start him on table food per schedule. At his six-month wellness check, the pediatrician called me out on it. They told me he was totally ready, and his gag reflex would improve with practice. The pediatrician gave me a handful of cheerios and watched as I nervously doled them out. Kids of all ages wake up in the middle of the night, stand at the side of your bed, and just as they're telling you they don't feel good, throw up all over you, the bedding, and the floor. I struggled.

I dreaded winter and the cold and flu season. I was criticized for my frequent use of hand sanitizer by those who didn't know or understand how that little hand pump gave me just enough reassurance that I could take my kids to the grocery store. There were no Chuck E. Cheese parties and very rarely restaurant play areas. Those would trigger my anxiety because I wouldn't be able to keep my kid's hands clean enough and definitely not out of their mouth.

There is a miracle amongst my struggles though, and that is, when any one of my kids actually did throw up, I was hands-on and focused on their discomfort, not mine. I was holding them, rubbing their back, cleaning the puke bucket, and washing the sheets. One, I didn't have much of a choice because my husband, more often than not, amazingly slept through all stomach-bug episodes—moms, how *does* that even happen?—two, I found that "the anticipation leading up to vomiting was worse than the actual vomiting" (Robinson 2023), and three, mom instinct is no joke. Even triggered and fighting my own fears, mom-mode automatically kicked in, and making them feel comfortable and safe instantly became my priority.

As Mia's stomachaches became more frequent, they also started to interfere with her living life as a first grader. She avoided playdates. She declined birthday parties unless I would go along. She loved soccer but struggled with the idea of being at practice alone, afraid of getting sick while there. Kids with emetophobia may "develop certain behaviors or avoid situations. It's common to experience anxiety around going to school. A lot of planning happens to avoid any possibility of vomiting in public" (Robinson 2023). We compromised. She would go to practice, and I would sit in the car in the parking lot with a book, Ty and Zoe with activity books, toys, or the ingenious invention of a portable TV/VHS player. It was enough reassurance for her to participate, and she never asked to leave practice once it started.

Because I knew what she was going through and desperately wanted to try and help her avoid missing out on "normal" activities and events that her peers enjoyed, I made it my mission to work hard with her early on. Our conversation when fear consumed her started with, "I know you are afraid." I always wanted to acknowledge her fear. "You are stronger than this fear"—empower her. "You like to play soccer and be with your friends"—remind her that this is something fun. "We will not let your fear stop you from doing something you like. You can do this, and I will help you." She is not alone.

I also felt it was time to find Mia a therapist.

Finding the right therapist is such a blessing for those trying to manage mental health struggles. Or for those who deeply love someone struggling. By now, I had confronted my own anxiety about throwing up and was working on managing it, but I desperately wanted to prevent my daughter from having to travel the same difficult and shameful path I had been on for far too long. And through her psychologist, Mia was given tools to use, diversion tactics to try, and I found an alliance.

"Hello, Mia, how was school today?" our doctor always greeted her with a smile and genuine interest. She sat down with Mia at a kid-sized table in her office while I sat on the couch. "Your mom was telling me that you had a hard time with school this week. That you had some worries. I was thinking that I'd like to show you something really special. Would you like that?"

I watched her draw my guarded daughter in, and Mia slowly shook her head yes. "These are some of my friends, and they're very special," she explained as she walked to a little box sitting on her windowsill, which she brought back to the table. "I call them worry monsters. They're not bad or mean monsters, though." She opened the lid to reveal a set of small, plastic finger puppets in varying colors, each with unique monsterlike features.

Mia was curious and now interested. "I want you to pick one out." Mia chose the red finger puppet.

"Oh, I like that one. That's a good choice. What should we name them?"

Mia thought a bit before replying, "I think… Mr. Red."

"Now, tell me one of the things you were worried about this week at school."

"I was worried I'd miss my mom," Mia shared.

"How did that make you feel, Mia?" The doctor offered her a safe space to talk.

"It made me sad. And it made my tummy hurt," Mia went on.

"I'm sorry about that. Let's try something. I want you to keep Mr. Red Worry Monster with you at school next week. Maybe keep him in your pocket or your desk. And when you start to worry about missing your mom, I want you to tell Mr. Red. Because guess what? Something special happens! Once Mr. Red knows about your worry, you don't have to worry about it anymore because it's *his* worry now and not yours." The doctor went on to have Mia name a second monster, giving that one her tummy ache worry. Mia proudly held those two in the palm of her little hand, and I was grateful to have a tool to work with in the coming weeks.

When days were really hard, our doctor became my partner in advocating for Mia but also my life raft.

"I'm struggling. I feel like a bad mom because Mia gets so frustrated and blows up at me. Ty and Zoe see it all, and I worry about what they'll grow up thinking is appropriate behavior. I can't have them talking back like Mia does. It doesn't seem like Mia cares if she hurts me. She yells and screams at me when she's angry. Then, the next time, she's worried about throwing up, or she's sad about missing me. She expects everything to be okay and for me to be loving and reassure her. It's like when she's over it, I'm just supposed to be over it, too, even though she's really hurt my feelings. It's hard to go back and forth emotionally like that. How do I teach her that I love her unconditionally but that it doesn't mean she's allowed to verbally abuse me and take advantage of that love?" I remember asking at one of our sessions during my one-on-one time.

"Deb, you are a very good mom. You are here, in therapy, with her because you love her. She doesn't want to hurt you. She doesn't want to be angry. She's a good kid, but she isn't in control of her emotions or reactions, which is what we are working to help her with. But you, you are a very good mom," she breathed hope into me. She became part of our weekly family. She listened not just to Mia but to me. She involved Ty and Zoe when appropriate, as therapy appointments and waiting rooms became part of their routine too. She was kind, patient, wise, and truly a blessing to our family as we would spend years visiting and working together.

Mia would struggle with overwhelm and task management for much of her life. Overstimulation, a strict schedule, tight deadlines, or being abruptly interrupted while hyper-focused would commonly send her into fight or flight mode. Lashing out or simply checking out and ignoring, for example, a "come down for dinner" or "I need you to unload the dishwasher right now" request. I recently read, "a child whose brain is in fight or flight looks a lot like a defiant child who won't listen. When our brain perceives we're under threat our body reacts in the same way as if we were truly in danger. This is anxiety. Our amygdala (brain's emotion center) is protecting us (as nature intended) through powerful survival instincts. When our brain's emotion center is over-activated (which is what happens with anxiety) a child is more inclined to be irritable and reactive as all emotions are working in overdrive" (Pruess 2022). The anxiety caused anger, and because she didn't understand what was going on yet and couldn't verbalize it to me, she flew into a rage.

I understood all too well my daughter's fear of getting sick, but I couldn't relate to the anger component that steadily got more intense. I struggled to remain patient. And I felt helpless as discipline in any form provoked rather than deterred her rage.

"Mia, if you don't stop calling your brother a stupid idiot, you're going to get soap in your mouth." Though I'm completely against this tactic now, I do remember threatening it in desperation, quickly finding it was ineffective.

"Fine! I'll put the soap in my own mouth," Mia would scream back at me.

"I have asked you twice to stop knocking over Zoe's princess castle and warned you that if you didn't stop, you would get a time-out. So go sit in the chair in the dining room until I come and talk with you." I tried. She would: (1) refuse to go, sitting stubbornly until I physically took her to the chair, (2) ignore me and start playing with Zoe's toys, or (3) stomp off to the dining room and scream and kick while sitting in the chair because she was angry and frustrated.

I also found preventing disobedience or outbursts a challenge because Mia lived very much for "right now." If on a Tuesday, I said, "Mia, I asked you to empty the dishwasher after dinner. You haven't done it yet, and you have been very disrespectful. If you don't do it in the next fifteen minutes, you will not be going to your friend's sleepover on Friday. I will set a timer," it would mean little to nothing to Mia. She would not empty the dishwasher and would continue to be disrespectful, causing her to lose the sleepover. And she wouldn't care. Until Friday, when the consequence was put into effect, and she wouldn't understand why she wasn't allowed to go. Even after reminding her, she would cry and scream that I was mean, unfair, and she hated me. I constantly felt like I was reacting instead of being proactive and as though I had no control over my kid. I was emotionally tired from being my daughter's biggest source of reassurance, while also being her verbal punching bag.

I look back now with a different mindset in a different stage of life, and sometimes I wish I parented differently or better, but that's unrealistic and unhealthy. I had a child who struggled with her mental health. I struggled with my own mental health. I was navigating unfamiliar waters with three little kids to manage, a home to run, and a great husband who was gone a lot. I did my best. I loved my best. I survived my best.

I am, however, so grateful for the therapy we sought out and started early on. It gave us the time necessary to establish a solid and safe relationship with someone whose experience and expertise would be fundamental in managing the health of Mia and our family. As she moved from first to second and on to third grade, Mia's anxiety and rage gained momentum. Having an established and trusted therapist in place when we were faced with one of the most terrifying scenarios a parent could navigate was a lifesaving gift.

LOVE HARD TIPS
How to Help a Child Struggling with a Fear of Throwing Up

1. "54321 Grounding Technique. Look for five things you can see, four things you can feel, three things you can hear, two things you can smell, and one thing you can taste. The brain must work hard to identify these items, distracting from the stronghold of the anxiety in that moment.
2. Explosion breathing. Start standing, breathe in, and crouch down at the same time, then jump up and spread arms and legs while breathing out.
3. Tear it up. Write out worries on paper, then rip the paper up. Acknowledging the anxious thoughts and feelings is important—and so is having the power to symbolically destroy those worries.
4. Fidget. Squeeze a squishy or use a designated fidget tool for distraction and calming.
5. Finger breathing. Pretend you're tracing a Thanksgiving turkey and slowly move up and down and in between each finger, taking deep breaths in and out along the way. This act is a meditation that takes focus and time to complete, redirecting the anxious feelings so they become more manageable" (Weiss 2023).

CHAPTER SEVEN

———

There is only one kind of shock worse than the totally unexpected: the expected for which one has refused to prepare.

—MARY RENAULT

"What did you just do!" I yelled to Mia as I ran across the yard to where she was standing. It happened so fast, my brain had yet to catch up to what my eyes just saw.

"Nothing," she calmly replied with a blank look on her face.

It was summer, two years later, and the kids were playing outside while I watched from our porch. In the blink of an eye, what had been a fun game of chase between Mia and Ty triggered her. She became angry at Ty and at the game. She couldn't catch him, and she flipped from carefree and joyful to enraged and vengeful. I watched her grab a rock from my garden—roughly the size of a football—scream, "I'm going to throw this rock at your head," and proceed to do so as he ran by her. It just barely missed him. Ty was unfazed, blissfully unaware of what could've happened.

There are moments in life so shocking, so unexpected, you aren't sure how to proceed. There is no manual and no training videos. Does one do a computer search for "What to do if my child throws a rock at my other child?" As an experiment, I did, in fact, Google exactly that recently, and do you know what came up? Links offering customized behavior charts, articles on "Discipline Rather than Punishment," and "How to Parent Positively." Though there is a time and place for those tools, we were way beyond the help of a brightly colored chart. Not to mention that back in 2009, there just wasn't the access to or quantity of parenting self-help as is the case today, nor was Google second nature to me. This situation had the potential to be deadly. I had to figure out a way to not only protect Ty but also Mia from her own impulsive actions.

I immediately brought Mia in from the yard and took her directly up to her room. Horrible scenarios were clouding my vision. "Do you know how badly you could've hurt your brother?" Where I should've removed her and then took a step back until I cooled off, I went charging ahead instead. "What were you thinking, throwing a rock at his head? I don't care how mad you are. You could've hurt or even killed him! Do you understand me?" I was scared and wanted her to be too. Instead, she sat on her bed, arms crossed, face set in a defensive scowl, almost daring me to punish her. "Violence is never appropriate and is not allowed. You will sit in your room until I come back and talk to you. While you're in here, I want you to write an apology letter to Ty," I finished before walking out and shutting the door behind me. I was shaking with fear and anger and knew I needed some space to regain control.

In that moment, I felt ashamed for not having control over my daughter's actions, not being able to protect my kid, and very much alone. Unlike when your child is sick, you don't call another mom-friend for advice in this situation. I couldn't even imagine what they would think or say. So I called Gary at work.

"Mia just threw a rock—a big rock—at Ty's head! They were outside playing. I was right there watching. She got mad at him and just picked it up and threw it! I'm so angry! And I'm so sad she acts like this. What could she have been thinking? And now what do I do with her?" I fumed.

I could hear Gary gasp.

"What! Where is she now?"

"In her room. I thought I was going to hit her; I was so upset! I needed to cool off so I told her to write him an apology, but when I was talking to her after it happened, it was like she was uninterested. Like she didn't care. She could've really hurt him, and she acted like it was no big deal!"

"I'll talk to her when I get home. I'm sorry you had to deal with this. Is Ty okay?"

"Yes, he and Zoe are still playing outside. I just don't know what to do. I'm upset, but I also don't want her to ever do something when she's mad and loses control and then have to live with it for the rest of her life. I want to protect all of them."

It's so hard to remain calm and reasonable when every one of your buttons are continuously pushed. You are well aware of how dire a situation is or could've been and your own first instinct is fight or flight. The battle that is fought as you try to keep your emotions in check and stay levelheaded when your emotionally charged reaction is to run away or, sadly, respond with violence yourself. When perhaps you should talk it out and calmly validate your child's emotions, the title of "mom" does not exempt you from still being human. You succumb to all the emotions—anger, frustration, hate—and then consciously work to always keep the child separate from the behavior. You are disappointed in the outburst, hate the actions, but you will always love your child.

Mia had just finished third grade, which marked two and half years spent working with her therapist. We continued to look for the magic formula to best manage—or better yet, cure—Mia's fear of throwing up. We had the tools, which included breathing techniques, worry monster figurines, countdown methods, and redirection strategies. But no matter how much we practiced them on days Mia's mood allowed us to, we still hadn't found the right approach. Stomachaches continued to plague her, but to make matters even more challenging, she was becoming more combative. Outbursts were extreme and frequently included threats of violence. The dynamic in our house was repeatedly volatile and unpredictable. Her triggers seemed to be people or things we couldn't remove or avoid altogether—her brother, her dad, rules, schedules. She would go from playing peacefully to irrational rage in seconds and without warning.

Understanding the dichotomy that is parenting a child who is both light and dark is hard. Mia was capable of such softness and joy. Her heart was good. She had a beautiful soul. She would write me notes saying, *"I love you, Mom. You're the best mom. I love you so much. You are awesome. Love is so important to me. Love, Mia."* I'd watch her play house with her babies, amazed and proud of the soft reassurances, tenderness when changing them, and kisses she'd give them. I'd see pieces of me in her and glimpses of the loving mom she might be one day. I'd see her on the soccer field, excitedly cheering on a teammate, laughing freely at a joke, proudly glancing my way when she scored a goal, and my heart would swell with incredible love. I'd catch her reading stories to her brother and sister, all snuggled up together like three peas in a pod. I loved the way her arms felt wrapped around me when she came to me tired or in need of healing kisses. She was wonderful.

But when the darkness of Mia's mental health was too powerful for her to control, she became cruel and unkind. I'd watch her, without warning, shove Ty to the floor and kick him because he was playing basketball in the hallway outside her bedroom. Verbal attacks were filled with hatred. I became emotionally numb when she'd lash out with, "I hate you and wish you were dead."

I dreaded car trips where all passengers were easy prey to her tirades. She'd start with taunts, "Ty, you're such a baby. I'm going to tell everyone at school you still suck your thumb," as he sat contentedly, thumb in mouth, looking out the window.

"Mom! Don't let her say anything," he'd react, panicked and embarrassed. Once she got a response, the insults just continued.

"You're stupid. You're such an idiot," she'd say, sensing weakness and striking again.

Those car episodes often occurred on the way home from school. After an entire day spent keeping her emotions in check and maintaining appropriate behavior, she was like an over-shook soda ready to explode. My mind understood that it took all her energy to perform in the classroom, but my heart wanted to protect the innocent bystanders. I couldn't allow her to be verbally abusive. I needed to teach her to have respect. I was also desperately trying to preserve the credibility of the guidelines we were teaching all three kids about what was right and wrong behavior.

Mia was in the battle of her life every day. The light and dark fighting each other for space and for attention. She had no control once she reached a specific point, and unfortunately, she reached it so quickly, we had little to no time to diffuse her and prevent harm. Mia wasn't choosing to be angry or choosing to lash out, "when children are under the influence of an anxious brain, their behavior has nothing to do with wanting to push against the limits. They are often great kids who don't want to do the wrong thing, but they are being driven by a brain on high alert" (Young 2023).

Many times, after a violent outburst, Mia would tell me she didn't remember what she did or why. She said the world went dark, and when the darkness cleared seconds or minutes later, she didn't know what had happened. At the time, and being undereducated myself, I thought she was making excuses by claiming ignorance. I've since learned that children struggling with mental health, whose behavior can be explosive and out of control, are more susceptible to what is called blind rage. "A blind rage is 'blind' in the sense the child may not be totally aware of his or her behavior during the rage episode. It's a feeling of intense and growing anger and driven more by anger-related issues and a need to retaliate. A child in a state of rage also loses much of his capacity for rational thought and reasoning, and may act (usually violently) on his impulses to the point he may attack until he has been restrained, or the source of his rage has been 'destroyed'" (Hutten 2013).

I appreciated and found incredible value in our therapy, but I believed Mia now required additional help. We needed to protect her from unintentionally doing something irrational and impulsive that would result in life-long, tragic consequences. My mission continued to be protecting her while also empowering her to take back control. I believed in the strength of her mind and trusted that if we found a way to manage her thoughts and emotions, she could live safer and happier—more adjusted. I wanted restfulness for her tightly wired brain.

"I talked with Mia's therapist at our session today, and she agreed it might help protect Mia and the kids if we started seeing a psychiatrist and explored medication to control her anger," I told Gary one evening after dinner. "I don't want her hurting someone. Doing something she would regret and pay for the rest of her life." I knew Gary was hesitant about medication, feeling at the time that much of the world was overmedicated and using it casually when unnecessary. But I needed and wanted him to be on board with this decision for it to have a chance.

"I don't want that either, but I also don't want her to be a zombie. Controlling her anger is one thing, but I don't want drugs to change her whole personality," he said. "But we've also tried everything, and it's not getting better. So, if you find a psychiatrist for her, I'll go with you."

I found the process of finding the right mental health professional emotionally challenging. Sharing your story, exposing your child, being vulnerable, and looking to feel a connection and hope, it's a dance. It's an intimate relationship. Lots of cogs need to work together to make the wheel spin smoothly. I put all my eggs into the basket of the first psychiatrist we met with. I needed him to help us and to help Mia. I hoped he would be the beacon of hope our family desperately needed.

We started sessions. Gary was involved and very much wanted to understand this next step. The doctor listened as we shared our challenges. He listened to Mia. He never gave us a diagnosis, but he prescribed meds. We noticed no change, which is not unusual when you're testing the waters of medication. We met some more, talked some more, and he made dosage changes. This time, her behavior got more aggressive, and she started gaining weight, which was a common side effect of one of the drugs he prescribed. We had more meetings and tried different meds. Again, no improvement. Gary grew doubtful, losing confidence in the doctor's competence. He liked his approach, demeanor, and drug suggestions less and less with every visit. I grew more frustrated and disheartened. I prayed with each medication change we'd find the magical combination, but we slowly lost hope.

We worked with that doctor for roughly a year until, at what would be our last session, he broke the news, "I just don't know what more I can do for Mia. What more can we try? Nothing seems to work." I stared at him blankly. Wait, are you saying she's a lost cause? Is my kid incapable of being helped? You're supposed to be the expert! Although we knew it was time to find someone else, it was devastating when he threw in the towel. I was crushed along with all those eggs I put in his basket.

The roller-coaster ride was falling headlong into a very dark and lonely place. It was not fun. It was not carefree. And it was not worth the price of admission. I wanted off. But I was still belted in alongside my daughter—for better or worse. All I could do was tighten my grip, close my eyes, and pray we would make it in one piece.

LOVE HARD TIPS
How to Respond to Your Child or Teen's Anger

1. "Don't Try to Control Your Child's Emotions. You can't control your child's emotions, and that's okay. But you can expect your child to control their behavior. So, do not ask, 'How do I prevent my child from getting angry?' Instead, ask, 'How do I get my child to behave appropriately when they get angry?'

2. Try to Control Your Own Emotions. A child's rage will often trigger a parent's own emotions. If you start experiencing intense emotion yourself, take a breath and a mental step back. One trick is to picture your child as a neighbor's kid. This can give you a little emotional distance.

3. Don't Escalate the Situation. Just because you choose not to argue with your child doesn't mean you're giving in. Give your child some space and time to cool down. If they're screaming at you, it's okay to wait to give a consequence. You can always hold your child accountable later on when things are calmer.

4. Help Your Child Recognize When Anger Is Building. There are physical signs of anger that your child can start to tune into: stomach clenching, a feeling of tension, feeling flushed, clenching teeth. If your child can notice these signs early on, it can keep anger from escalating to rage.

5. Talk about the Incident. When you are both calm, talk about the incident. Many kids will experience or express genuine remorse after having an emotional meltdown. If they're open to talking and willing to learn anger management skills, you can help them work backward from the incident. What happened right before the rage was triggered? What was said? What were they feeling? Embarrassment, frustration, disappointment, fear, anxiety?

6. Remember That Emotion Is Different from Behavior. The problem isn't the anger; it's the behavior that follows. You can validate your child's emotions while addressing the behavior that is a concern. You can say this to your child: *"I understand you were angry when I said you couldn't go to your friend's house. Sometimes there will be rules or limits that may frustrate you, but breaking things won't change*

that rule or limit and will only end in a consequence for that behavior." Then help your child identify more positive ways they can express their emotions.

7. Minimize Contributing Factors. The way your child perceives a situation is at the heart of anger. However, you may want to keep a calendar on their mood if it seems things are escalating. Do they tend to be more irritable if they don't get enough sleep, skip meals, have poor eating habits, or otherwise aren't feeling well physically?

8. Managing Explosive Rage. Some parents worry because a child's anger is beyond what they would consider typical. If your child's anger is extreme, you may want to seek counseling. Even if your child won't participate, you can go yourself to get support and guidance. No matter what degree of anger your child exhibits, the fact is, they're still responsible for managing that emotion" (Abraham and Cordner 2023).

Book Recommendations for Kids

1. *What to Do When Your Temper Flares: A Kid's Guide to Overcoming Problems with Anger* by Dawn Huebner
2. *Way Past Mad* by Hallee Adelman
3. *I Love You When You're Angry* by Karen Winters

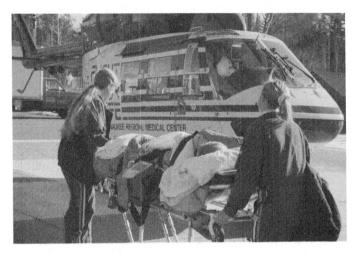

My Flight For Life ride from the Northwoods. They said I was too high
risk to take a normal medical transport plane.
(photo courtesy Deborah Mueller)

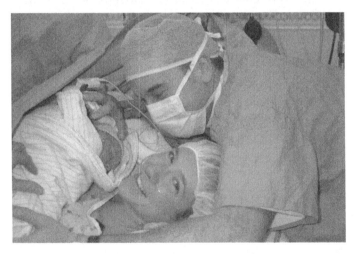

Delivery day of our healthy baby girl. One of the best days of our lives.
(photo courtesy Deborah Mueller)

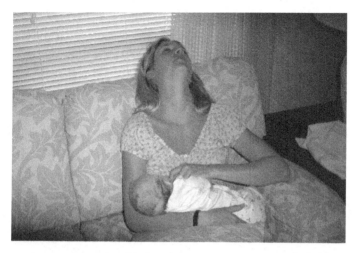

The early days of exhaustion. (photo courtesy Deborah Mueller)

Gary took turns with Mia whenever possible so I could get some sleep.
(photo courtesy Deborah Mueller)

Once out of the crib, Mia never stayed in her bed.
(photo courtesy Deborah Mueller)

There were lots of happy days too.
(photo courtesy Deborah Mueller)

The exhaustion and interrupted sleep continues.
(photo courtesy Deborah Mueller)

Daddy's girl.
(photo courtesy Deborah Mueller)

Our first chart to reward positive behavior.
(photo courtesy Deborah Mueller)

Trying a new reward chart style to encourage happier mornings.
(photo courtesy Deborah Mueller)

A car ride tantrum at it's finest.
(photo courtesy Deborah Mueller)

My growing family.
(photo courtesy
Deborah Mueller)

A storm is brewing in those eyes.
(photo courtesy Deborah Mueller)

Another incentive chart for positive behavior. (photo courtesy Deborah Mueller)

Sensory issues and sensitivity led to Mia's boy clothes phase. (photo courtesy Deborah Mueller)

I cherished the tiny moments of peace and kindness.
(photo courtesy Deborah Mueller)

Proud parents on High School graduation day from Living Word.
(photo courtesy Deborah Mueller)

Final goodbyes on college move-in day. Even though she wasn't far away, it was still hard. (photo courtesy Deborah Mueller)

Proud to be back living on her own #apartmentliving. (photo courtesy Deborah Mueller)

College graduation day with our family celebrating Mia. She did it!
(photo courtesy Deborah Mueller)

Her future is bright! (photo courtesy Deborah Mueller)

CHAPTER EIGHT

———

You will look back on therapies, appointments, sleepless nights, tears, triumphs, milestones, equipment, ignorance, struggle, strength, and you'll say with certainty... it was absolutely worth it.

—UNKNOWN

I was losing myself to parenting. It's a thankless job that I wouldn't trade for anything in the world.

I felt it. I knew it. I allowed it. My kids consumed me with their lives, their activities, their struggles, and their needs. There is a fine line when loving becomes unhealthy, and that's when it's at the expense of one's needs.

Nothing fills you and drains you quite like being a parent.

Two more years had passed, and Gary and I were growing apart—slowly and subtly. We picked more arguments with each other because we were both preoccupied with other stressors, me with the kids and him with work. When we spent time one-on-one, we were really good. Quick getaways and dinner dates probably helped save us. But that wasn't the real, everyday world. And it became easy to coexist. Each of us were individually handling our household contributions and not working together on many things.

I felt unseen and resentful that Mia's extensive mental health and school needs fell solely on my shoulders, save a few doctor visits, along with all other house and kid responsibilities. Gary was frustrated at having to give more when he got home from work at night, after giving all day to clients and coworkers. He and I had little patience left by the time 7 p.m. rolled around, which was the perfect atmosphere for short tempers and conflict.

"Deb, you've got to be kidding me! You know I can't be at every appointment. I have a job! And that job pays for everything, including Mia's therapy," he'd angrily chastise when pressed.

"Don't talk down to me! I am not one of your employees. And, I am well aware of how great your job is. I'm just asking for a little help," I'd defensively respond. Eventually, we'd both retreat to our own corners, issue unsolved and hostility thick in the air.

There was seemingly never any time to work on us. We were surviving. The state of continuing to live or exist, typically in spite of an accident, ordeal, or difficult circumstances. This would mark the first of many years where survival became my main objective. I was preserving my happiness, preserving the strength of our family, preserving Mia's reputation among her teachers, peers, and family members, preserving my marriage, preserving the childhoods of Ty and Zoe, and preserving my very emotionally fragile relationship with Mia. I was balancing many delicate plates, trying to keep them all spinning, having yet to learn that we can't be all things to all people, and we cannot keep all the plates in the air all the time. Sometimes a plate has to fall.

I poured myself into finding a new psychiatrist for Mia. Just like starting in the first place, starting over is hard too— forms, insurance, scheduling, interviews to determine a good fit, being vulnerable, respeaking the unspeakable. This time I was no fool. I was guarded. I was not hopeful but skeptical. My eggs were all tucked safely in their carton on a shelf in my fridge.

When we finally found a match, meaning a doctor who came highly recommended and was taking new clients, it was not an immediate connection for Mia.

I recently asked Mia, "When you met Dr. R, did you like him right from the start? I can't remember."

She replied, "Hmm, no, I didn't like him at first. But I didn't like anyone back then. Eventually though, I got more comfortable with him, and he actually was my favorite therapist."

This new doctor was calm, thoughtful, and insightful. He listened well, and when he spoke, it was with intention. He had years of experience. Shortly after meeting him, I felt safe exposing my own insecurities about being an incompetent mom and sharing examples of Mia's aggressive and violent behavior. "Deb, you are not incompetent. You are here getting the help Mia needs. That's wisdom. That's love," he reassured. He never judged, always greeted Mia with a smile and kindness, and seemed to be unshockable, which was paramount if we were to have an ongoing open and honest relationship. We began weaning Mia off certain meds while adding in new ones, still trying to find the right combination. The process was tedious and slow as we had to do it one at a time to best evaluate the effects.

Through the transition of a psychiatrist and medication changes, we were also tasked to navigate one of the most difficult years of school. The fifth grade happened. If you know, you know, right mamas?

Kids were being challenged to be more academically independent in preparation for middle school the following year. That small bit of freedom was overwhelming to Mia. She started forgetting to bring home assignments, often telling me she had no homework when she most certainly did. She put off studying for tests until the night before and then panicked at the overwhelm of information she was required to learn. Her notes were done poorly or missing altogether, which made studying incredibly difficult.

I found myself coming to her rescue often, helping her study at the last minute and asking for grace when assignments were forgotten. My hope was for her to avoid the inevitable bad grade she'd get and possible sports ineligibility. The problem was, she wasn't learning how to become more self-sufficient, she wasn't dealing with the consequences that came with not being prepared, and she wasn't doing the work.

It was easier for her to take advantage of the grace she was given by me and her teachers.

I decided it was time to try a little tough love. In my effort to make schoolwork more comfortable, I had enabled her to become lazy. Her teachers and I would now work together, allowing her to suffer the consequences of incomplete or missing assignments just like her peers. I still helped her study for tests and quizzes, but she had to work with me nightly, going over notes she intentionally took time to take during class, as opposed to cramming the night before. If she refused to work with me, then she was on her own. I hoped this approach might motivate her to work harder and more independently. We were on the cusp of middle school, where even less handholding was permitted, and she would be expected to take ownership of her work to succeed.

I talked about it with Mia, loosened the reins, and let her fly solo. With each zero for missing work and failing grade, her anxiety spiked. The stress over doing poorly brought on more stomachaches, which triggered her fear of throwing up, which resulted in more outbursts that were followed by a "Whatever, I don't care anyway" attitude. It was the classic fight-or-flight response. Her body was preparing her to react or to retreat for survival.

"Mia, what's going on with your schoolwork?" I asked when she was calm and seemed receptive to talking. "You know that you're smart. And I know that you're capable of getting homework turned in on time. So, I don't understand why you have missing assignments. Remember, we agreed that I was going to back off and not bother you so much because you said you wanted to do it on your own. Now, your grades are down, and I feel like you've been even angrier lately."

"I don't know. I thought I could do it, but now I'm just always so worried. I don't remember to bring my assignments home, and then I feel bad and start to feel pressure. I get extra nervous that you're not helping me, and then I think I'm going to fail and that I might not be able to play volleyball or you and Dad will be mad at me," Mia confided.

"Okay. I get that. I don't want you to fail or be nervous and worried. I'm happy to help you, but we need to work as a team." I wanted to empower, not enable her.

Shortly after our talk, Mia and I met with her therapist to discuss what had been happening at school and how it was making her feel. We agreed Mia was not a child prepared to be totally self-sufficient at this stage in the game. We decided she would start by owning a smaller subject—her memory work. She would be in charge of those regular assignments and suffer smaller consequences that had lower stress levels attached to them.

Now let's talk about studying. It was a nightmare. Mia was easily distracted, which made it necessary for me to isolate her in a quiet room and sit with her as she learned information. I chose our dining room off the kitchen so I could also be in the near vicinity of Ty and Zoe. Even with the help of flashcards and study games, she was often pacing the room or laying upside down on a chair while I was going over material with her. If I had to step out of the room to start dinner or attend to Ty and Zoe, leaving her to briefly study independently, it wouldn't be unusual for me to return and find the contents of her binder or backpack emptied onto the table or floor. Mia, now distracted, would be focused on reorganizing her belongings instead of studying the notes we had been going over.

At home and at school, the anxiety about throwing up continued. Mia had stomachaches daily—often in the morning and always before bed. I was getting more calls from her while at school, sometimes two or three a day. During volleyball games, she'd frantically wave down the coach needing to be rotated out because her stomach hurt, and she was afraid of throwing up. The pressure of tests, serving a volleyball, and a forgotten assignment all made her stomach hurt, which triggered her fear of vomiting, which resulted in panic.

I knew it was time for me to let a few people in on her struggles and treatment. To work best with her, they needed to better understand her. Her coach created a "take me out of the game quickly" signal Mia could use to avoid as much unnecessary attention as possible. The principal greeted her warmly whenever she was in the office. Mia's teachers showed her grace by letting her leave class to go to the bathroom or to call me, no questions asked, if her stomach hurt. The school secretary waived the twenty-five-cent phone charge and always let her call me for reassurance. I cannot say enough about the incredible blessing our school family was as they worked alongside me to accommodate and empower Mia.

This same year, Mia developed sensory processing difficulties. "For the estimated 5 to 15 percent of school-aged children affected, the world is simply too much. Too loud. Too bright.

Food is either too soft or too crunchy. The labels and seams on clothes too scratchy. SPD is a genuine physiological condition that affects how their central nervous system processes input from their senses, leaving them under- or over-responsive to stimuli. It can significantly affect a child's behavior at home and school. When kids are working overtime to try to regulate their senses, their behavior isn't always exemplary. At school, they may disrupt the class or struggle to concentrate on lessons" (Green 2016).

Tags bothered her. Material bothered her. She began wearing her brother's T-shirts because they were looser and more comfortable and eventually asked for her own boy-categorized wardrobe. Swim shorts and swim shirts replaced her one-piece. T-shirts and shorts from the boy's section were her preference. Sporty sweatsuits were a staple in the winter. I grew protective, worried about the day she walked in wearing the same outfit as one of the boys in her class. Remarkably, her classmates didn't pay her evolving style much attention. She was still simply, Mia. A direct testament to the amazing families of the kids in Mia's class and the kindness and acceptance taught at our Christian school.

Our bedtime routine often lasted over an hour. Mia would have hysterical fits about being afraid, being alone, or getting sick. There was excessive bargaining, stomping, wailing, and stalling. The bedtime routine consisted of hall lights on, music on, closet light on, blankets selected, night light on, lava lamp on, glass of water and cracker on nightstand, allotted books chosen and set by bed, drapes pulled, door open—or maybe closed halfway—nope, open, kisses given, prayers said, and "you are not going to throw up" reassurances spoken.

The rituals and hoops we jumped through were exhausting. By evening, I was desperate for the day to be over and went through the motions robotically.

Once, while chaperoning a field trip with a few other moms and talking about our fifth-grade girls, I listened as my friend shared with us how much she loved the bedtime routine she had with her daughter. They would read together for a bit, and then, because it was just the two of them and quiet, her daughter would tell her all about the day she had as they snuggled close. I knew she wasn't trying to make me feel bad. She had no idea what was going on in my home at night because I fiercely protected us from possible judgment by staying quiet. But I vividly remember being envious of the ease of their routine and relationship.

The aggression continued as well. Shouting was our morning routine. I've since learned there is a connection between ADHD and explosive behavior. As reported on by Dr. Vinay Saranga, "It's really about poor frustration tolerance and the inability to control emotions. This is often why they lash out. Getting ready for school involves a lot of individual steps. You have to choose your clothes, eat breakfast, get dressed, pack up your school bag, maybe make a lunch, and be ready at the door. Add ADHD to that mix, and dealing with all those pieces in the morning can be overwhelming" (Saranga 2019).

Gary was often on school drop-off duty because it aligned with his work schedule. Ty was in second grade, and Zoe was in kindergarten. They both loved school. They were up and dressed on their own, often laughing and bantering at the breakfast table while I made lunches. When Mia joined them, in many cases angry and confrontational, the dynamic changed, requiring me to separate her from them. They were easy prey, and any reaction she'd get would feed her anger. Their breakfast finished, Ty and Zoe would get their bags ready, brush their teeth, and head to Gary's truck with quick kisses and hugs goodbye all while Mia was dragging her feet and fighting me about going to school.

"I don't want Dad taking me to school! I hate Dad! I want you to take me!" Mia screamed at me one morning.

"Mia, get in the truck. Your brother and sister are already out there and will be late for school, and so will you. Dad is taking you and that's final." I was so tired of the conflict and starting my days with anger. I just needed her to go to school. She became more enraged, screaming, stomping her feet, kicking her backpack, and refusing to walk out the door.

"I have a meeting; we have to go Mia. Get in the car." Gary was running late. To help the process along, I half dragged and half carried her to his truck and set her in the back seat.

"I love you, and I'm sorry you're angry. I will see you after school," I said through clenched teeth.

When I got back to our front door and turned around to wave, I saw that Gary had stopped further down our dead-end road. Mia, half in and half out, was trying to crawl through the small sliding back window of his truck. I watched as she climbed back inside the truck, only half caring about how he got her to comply but relieved he did.

When I say that our goal became keeping Mia and her siblings safe when she became consumed with rage, I mean it with my entire being. There were many incidents when reasoning, warnings, countdowns, calm talking, embraces, and kisses were simply ineffective. In dangerous situations, we were taught to use restraint. Wrapping her in arms of strength and love while repeating the words "you are okay, you are safe, you are loved," as she kicked and spit at us. It was emotionally painful, but we believed it was necessary to keep her from jumping out a window or moving vehicle, punching a family member, or destroying property. Do I know restraint isn't ideal or socially acceptable? Absolutely. Were we working with mental health professionals who advised us on techniques, the logic behind them, and reviewed each scenario with us afterward? Yes. Would I do it again to keep my child or children safe? A thousand times yes.

I continued to feel such shame and embarrassment about myself as a mom, my parenting, and my inability to help Mia—fix her, discipline her, understand her, or control her. As well as the absenteeism I felt with Ty and Zoe because of all the time spent with and for Mia. You ask yourself what am I doing wrong? What could I do better or differently?

What I did believe with all my heart was that God chose Mia for me and me for Mia. Being her mom pushed, stretched, and challenged me. I had to parent uniquely, creatively, and strategically with unconditional love, heart, and armor.

"Motherhood changes you. And because of that you must redefine who you are despite all the responsibilities that come with being a mom. The key is to not allow the pursuit of being a good mother rob you of the importance of being kind to yourself as well. Make sure you prioritize your needs right up there with every other commitment. By doing so, you will be giving your kids and your spouse a wonderful gift—a woman who not only likes who she is but also knows herself well enough to respect what she needs from life" (Gordon 2020).

LOVE HARD TIPS
Ten Tips for Overwhelmed Moms

1. "Acknowledge What You're Feeling. The only thing worse than the bitterness you're feeling is the mom guilt that comes with it. Take time to acknowledge what you're feeling—even journal about it. Then validate these feelings, and tell yourself you're doing the best you can, because you are!
2. Build or Find a Community and Ask for Help. Asking for help is a sign of strength, not weakness. Build or find a community of friends or fellow moms who can help you with the big stuff and the small stuff.
3. Clear Your Plate. When you look at your schedule, it probably won't be obvious what to cut out. Just because something isn't bad doesn't mean it's good for you. Having your schedule too full prevents you from enjoying any of your commitments! Practice saying "no."
4. Practice Gratitude. Try a gratitude journal or, if you're spiritual, try praying over your blessings or meditating on things you're thankful for.
5. Prioritize Self-Care. Self-care can feel selfish and like a waste of time, but it is one of the most integral pieces to your health and sanity! Remember, taking time to

recharge will give you the positivity, patience, and insight to better enjoy your days and be the best mom you can be. You could journal, meditate, read a book, craft, or even go for a drive! Find something that gives you peace and fulfillment.

6. Wake Before the Kids. Consider rising before your children to get ready, grab some coffee, and maybe spend a little time planning your afternoon activity.

7. Don't Compromise Your Sleep. When looking at your schedule, it might look like sleep is the easiest thing to cut back on to keep the house tidy and the laundry put away. Your sleep is vital to your mental health, and your needs matter, too, so make sure you're getting in those eight hours of sleep.

8. Spend Time with Friends. Spending time with friends reminds you that you're a person with an identity that's more than just "mom." Obviously, your role as a mom is an incredible part of you, but there is more to you the world likely doesn't see if you're depriving yourself of your social needs.

9. Get Outside. Getting outside to go for a walk or work will help improve anxiety, mood swings, sleep, and even appetite problems! Spending just fifteen minutes outside a day will greatly improve your mental health and relieve that feeling of burnout.

10. Take a Break. You are allowed to take care of yourself. Don't feel guilty for taking some time away from the kids to breathe and recharge. Get away for the evening or for the weekend with your partner or by yourself or have a mini-vacation with your girlfriends. Whatever it is, put it on the calendar and give yourself a much-need and *much*-deserved break" (Pratt 2023).

CHAPTER NINE

———

What we don't need in the midst of struggle is shame for being human.

—BRENÉ BROWN

"I hate you! I want to kill myself! I'm going to the basement and getting Dad's gun, and I'm gonna kill myself!" Mia screamed as she ran through the living room toward the basement door.

She was frantic. Her eyes were wild.

Gary followed Mia downstairs, where he found her manically pacing and still screaming through gritted teeth. She was simmering with rage, her body electric, her hands clenched. He took her into his arms, pulled her down to the floor and into his lap and held her tightly, while repeating, "You are safe. You are okay." Tears streamed down his face as she fought against him. Her pain and struggle became his.

Holding her this way was beneficial in two ways. It reinforced his love but offered her protection. "When older children are dangerous to themselves and others, and behavioral techniques aren't enough to keep them, and others around them, safe, learning how to use safe holds may help keep both them and yourself out of harm's way" (Child Mind Institute 2023).

As she sagged into Gary's arms, her rage quieting and body yielding to his embrace, she became remorseful and apologetic. The older she got, the more aware she became of how she behaved. Deflated and exhausted, she asked Gary, "Why did God even make me, and why did He give me all these problems?" Another gut punch to her already emotional dad, and not uncommon in kids with aggressive tendencies due to anxiety and even sensory processing issues. As written about on the Family Resource Center blog, "kids who have trouble handling their emotions can lose control and direct their distress at a caregiver, screaming and cursing, throwing dangerous objects, or hitting and biting. It can be a scary, stressful experience for you and your child, too. Children often feel sorry after they've worn themselves out and calmed down" (Child Mind Institute 2023).

This was the summer of 2012. We were hosting a high school boy from Germany for a week who had been introduced to us by Gary's oldest daughter. She was twenty-seven and living in Berlin, Germany, at the time. To give him a taste of America, we took him boating and waterskiing, to waterparks and amusement parks, enjoyed cookouts, backyard baseball games, and soccer at the park. The kids adored him; they were fascinated by his accent and taste of music. He was a talkative, interesting, and well-mannered guest, and it was fun to see our country through his eyes.

Mia was twelve and headed into seventh grade. Adolescence added additional fuel to the flames of her anxiety and temper, but we continued to work on her behavior alongside her therapist and with medication. One afternoon, as our exchange student sat alongside Ty, now ten, and Zoe, now seven, watching TV, I heard Mia start yelling from her room upstairs. Sensing a storm brewing, I prayed I could calm her down and avoid exposing our very unsuspecting guest to what could potentially become a loud and violent outburst.

"Hey Mia, I can tell you're angry. You're being really loud up here. What's going on? What happened?" I asked, stepping inside her bedroom and closing the door. "I don't think we want our friend downstairs to be scared or worry about you being angry. Will you please try and quiet down so we can talk about this?" I was met with anger and more yelling. She had been triggered, and the switch flipped. She continued to escalate. My attempts to distract her and redirect her emotions were actually making her more upset. Hoping to avoid making things any worse, I chose to remove myself and go back downstairs.

A minute or two later, she charged down the stairs, screaming threats of violence and continued to the basement with Gary close behind.

"What is going on? Oh my gosh! Is she getting a gun? That was so messed up!" Our exchange student was terrified.

"Will she get a gun? Is she going to shoot someone? Are you going to stop her? This is seriously so messed up!"

He was looking to me for answers, pacing and nervously running his hands through his hair.

Ty's eyes briefly watched his friend then quickly returned back to the show on TV. Sadly, he was accustomed to Mia's threats and anger and no longer as reactive. Zoe, being younger and still more sensitive, was crying. She was scared for Mia's safety and by our friend's reaction. I scooped her up in my arms, wishing once again that I was able to shield her young heart better.

"When Mia gets angry, it takes control of her. She says lots of things she doesn't mean, and I know it's scary. Gary's with her downstairs, and she's safe. You are safe. She's not going to get a gun. I'm very sorry this happened, but she is not going to hurt anyone." I tried to reassure our friend. I couldn't believe we had gotten to a place where I was seemingly "blowing off" a death threat having been down this road many times before. Knowing it was rage and not Mia in control.

Later, I emailed our exchange student's mom. I needed to fill her in and somehow explain the unexplainable while reassuring her that her son was still safe in our care. Selfishly, I wanted to protect Mia, but I knew, in this case, it was necessary to expose her—to explain her. I needed to take the risk of being judged as a mom, and I knew she could not possibly understand what had become customary in our home. After receiving my message, she responded—concerned but kind. She was appreciative that I made her aware and wanted to talk with her son more about it.

Exposing Mia that day was emotionally hard. I kept much of her struggles and behavior to myself. Safe within the walls of our home and family. I found the few times I opened the door and trusted someone enough to share my secrets, people were eager to chime in with advice on how to raise my daughter. With the right community, women lift each other up. On the other hand, women can also be incredibly hard on each other. Many swearing, "My child will *never* behave that way" or "I would never allow that behavior," as they watch another mom's battle and despair. They are able to talk confidently, having no idea what the road is like.

For instance, when I mentioned we were contemplating medication for Mia, I was given articles on how the United States was overmedicating kids, using drugs instead of alternative therapies, and given tips on holistic approaches from a family friend in her twenties with no partner or kids.

Another friend offered up, "Don't take this the wrong way, but I think you're falling into a very common trap. You're labeling her and really just making excuses for her behavior."

I was told, "You give in too often and need to be more consistent with discipline. The follow through is key," from a mom who had kids who did respond to time-outs and the loss of privileges.

"I say this with love, but I think you're allowing Mia to take advantage of you. She's manipulating you to do whatever she wants. When she misbehaves and you give her attention, even if it's yelling at her, you are rewarding her and creating an unhealthy pattern. You need to ignore her outbursts," a woman in a mom's group advised, having never witnessed Mia's violence toward her own self or others.

I think what hurt the deepest though was when I heard, "I don't know what you're talking about, Deb. She never does that at my house. She's always well-behaved and listens. She's such a good girl," when I shared that I was struggling with her being violent or defiant. Instead of feeling grateful that Mia could hold it together when with others, my shame and insecurity kicked in. It reaffirmed that I must be the problem and parenting wrong if she was only misbehaving with me.

Over the years, I would be advised to try different methods of discipline by friends, family, books, and speakers. Many would tell me to enforce better boundaries, spank, take things away, don't take things away, take only certain things away, talk more, talk less, don't speak with anger, speak with authority and demand respect, ignore her, pay her more attention, let her have more choices, and let her have less choices. Though they were well-meaning, all this did was add to my already overwhelming feelings of failure and self-doubt, reminding me that silence and pretending were safer. Most of them didn't know we were trying all the things at the advice of our therapists. And guess what? All the things weren't working.

Mia's outbursts continued to be frequent if not daily. Babysitters would call us to come home from dates, fearing she would follow through on threats to hurt herself or Ty. She would become violent if a board game didn't result in her winning, if Ty or Zoe didn't play baseball in the yard according to her rules, if a TV program wasn't her choice, if she was told to stop playing and get ready for bed, or if her siblings had a toy she wanted.

The picture of irony, as much as I believed Mia craved control, her bedroom was always the picture of chaos. Clothes both clean and dirty, along with toys, crafts, and any other items she owned were strewn across the floor. Dresser drawers were pulled open. Piles of papers, clothes, and jewelry were on all the surfaces. Any efforts to have her conform to my desire for her room to be in order and clean were a waste of time. It was just another battle, and one I eventually chose to give up. I found it interesting when her psychiatrist told me the reason her room looked as though a tornado had just blown through was because it mirrored how her brain worked. Her thoughts, emotions, and impulses were all over the place, swirling around in a mess. He reminded me that she didn't "choose" to be a messy kid, just like she didn't "choose" to have a brain filled with agitation. In fact, it was exhausting for her.

The rare times I'd put my foot down and tell her to clean her room, her therapist advised me to give her notice. "Mia, today your chore is cleaning up just the floor of your room. I don't want you or me to trip over anything. I will give you thirty more minutes to play with your dolls, and then you need to start picking up," I'd warn and follow up with a countdown reminder so she knew what was coming and when. Asking Mia to do a chore "right now" was a trigger. She needed time to mentally prepare and advance notice to transition to the new task. Being smart, she figured out if she gave a bunch of her toys to Zoe in a gesture of kindness, she could get her room cleaned up much more quickly. Zoe was always an eager recipient of her unexpected gifts. The problem was, this was only a temporary fix in Mia's mind. When she'd see Zoe playing with those toys a few days later, she'd fly off the handle and grab them back, confusing and devastating her younger sister.

Time-outs in her bedroom were often our go-to discipline tactic. By removing us and our words from her space, she could begin to refocus on herself and, in fact, self-distract. "When a child is getting physical, ignoring them is not recommended since it can result in harm to others as well as your child. In this situation, put the child in a safe environment that does not give them access to you or any other potential rewards" (Child Mind Institute 2023). It was a safe place for her to yell and scream it out and then regroup. It was a space where she would find distraction and gain composure. I had to manage her safety while also managing what Ty and Zoe were witnessing, scared of, confused about, and learning. What often followed Mia's rage was an uncanny calm. In time, her room would grow quiet, and when I'd go to check on her, more often than not, she was playing dolls calmly and sweetly, or organizing her closet.

She'd greet me with a smile and a "Hi, Mom!" as though the emotional tornado never happened.

"What are you doing up here, Mia?" I'd cautiously ask.

"Just playing," she'd reply.

Unless the time spent in her room backfired. Once, I came up to find a hole the size of a small cantaloupe in her wall. I asked Mia more recently about the incident, and she recalled, "Yes, I remember being in my room. I was angry about something at first. I don't remember what it was. But then I remember being bored. So, I laid on my bed and started kicking the wall. Then I was curious if I could actually make a hole in the wall, and I kept kicking harder and harder until I did. I kicked a hole in the wall." A few weeks later, she learned how to drywall and paint that wall with her grandpa, while they fixed the hole together. When remembering and discussing other times she spent regrouping in her room, she shared, "I also remember being sent to my room when I was angry, and I chose to jump on that wooden toy box I had. It felt good. And, I just kept jumping until it broke."

My daughter's brain was wired differently. Her obsession was big as was her anxiety, which caused her emotions to be big as well. She felt deeply. She loved big, worried big, and was angry big. Her rage was a symptom of her anxiety, and her anxiety truly "like a roller coaster, terrifying and stressful, and to those that suffer from it, it never seems to stop. Imagine trying to write a letter on a roller coaster. Or cook a meal. Or sleep" (Fuller 2020). Nothing constructive was possible while the ride was running. Mia had no control. And we all just had to hold on and make it through the extreme highs and lows alongside her.

Our ride was still flying through the dark tunnels of mental health. There were moments of light as we moved from one track to the next, but we were still a long way from feeling the relief and joy we hoped would greet us at the end.

LOVE HARD TIPS
What to Say to a Parent of a Child with Mental Illness

1. "Acknowledge the Pain of Mental Illness. Saying you're sorry to hear about a child's specific mental health struggle makes the parent feel heard and validated. It gives them permission to open up and talk more about their child's mental illness if they choose to. Try saying any of the following:
   a. I'm sorry to hear that.
   b. It must be hard for you.
   c. I'm here for you.
   d. How are things going?
   e. Let's do coffee.
2. Show Empathy and Compassion for a Parent of a Child with Mental Illness. Acknowledge that their situation sounds extremely difficult. Remind them that you will be there for them, figuratively and literally.
3. Ask Questions, Listen, and Be Respectful. By asking questions, you show you care and you are interested in how the parent is doing. They may tell you too much information or not want to talk about it at all, but either way, it mattered to them that you asked.
4. Offer to Do Things with a Parent of a Child with Mental Illness. Sometimes they need a break, and this provides them the opportunity to take one.
5. Offer Advice Only If Requested. Most of the time, moms simply need a loving, listening ear. Unless you are asked

for it or a qualified professional, it's best to keep your tips and tricks to yourself.

6. Never Judge or Criticize. You may think you understand, but chances are high that you don't. And truly, it's not your place to judge or criticize how another mom parents as long as she is doing it with love" (Halli 2015).

CHAPTER TEN

———

The kids who need the most love will ask for it in the most unloving ways.

—RUSSELL BARKLEY

"Mama, do you love me?" Mia asked one night of her eighth-grade year.

It was bedtime. The routine from hell. It had been a hard day, and I was tired. I didn't want to be touched or needed or asked to do one more thing. I just wanted space.

"Yes, Mia, I love you," I automatically replied while pulling the shades.

"Do you love Ty and Zoe more than me?" Mia continued. I stopped because her voice was soft and vulnerable. There was no hostility, no accusation, and no anger. I moved to the bed and sat down next to her.

"Why do you ask?" I questioned, genuinely curious.

"Because you never yell at them, but I always get yelled at for being bad."

As the mom of a child battling mental health, I battled my own demons every day. The monster made it near impossible to be both loving and light while remaining cautious, skeptical, and protective. Not every minute or hour was traumatic or tumultuous. In fact, much of every day was by definition "typical." There was playing dress up, adventures in the yard, sandbox creations, coloring, Legos, and Playmobil. Mia, Ty, and Zoe did, in fact, play well together—entertaining themselves with crafts, books, and make believe. Those moments of normalcy made the outbursts somehow more difficult to handle. When I'd let my guard down, lose myself in the moments of joy and togetherness, I lost my edge. I allowed myself to be blindsided and disappointed when the environment suddenly became fraught with anger and abuse.

I also battled the guilt that came with how easy it was to show my love to Ty and Zoe when showing my love to Mia required much more planning and work. She craved loving gestures but was less receptive, less approachable, and frequently combative. Let me be clear so as not to confuse anyone. I am not saying I loved any of my children more or less. I am saying loving Ty and Zoe was like water skiing on two skis, while loving Mia was like slaloming. I absolutely love skiing both ways, but one is more challenging. It requires greater skill, practice, and stamina. And she saw it. She was smart and aware. In her mind, she was always getting yelled at while her brother and sister were getting all my love.

And in a sense, I saw her point. Because we were curbing, stopping, or addressing harmful behavior regularly. And so much was trial and error as we worked alongside her therapists. We tried positive reinforcement. I attended a parenting conference through our church hosted by a woman trained in the "Love and Logic" approach to parenting. The course was based on the book, *Parenting with Love and Logic* by Jim Fay and Foster Cline. I worked to implement its five principles, "using humor and empathy to build up our adult/child relationship while emphasizing respect and dignity for both and providing limits in a loving way" (Love and Logic Institute 2023). I joined a good friend two years in a row at a weekend retreat for moms, hoping to glean parenting ideas from the keynote speakers and breakout sessions. We tried charts, stickers, and prizes as incentives and praise for positive behavior. Unfortunately, none of those tactics or approaches worked consistently, if at all, to diffuse or prevent blow-ups or minimize her anxiety.

On top of it, Mia was unaffected by threats, our disappointment, or our anger. If anything, being challenged made a situation ten times worse. We took away toys and privileges, which made her initially angry, but soon she'd move on, seemingly unaffected. Friends of ours suggested having her work off disrespectful or hurtful behavior alongside Gary. Picking up sticks in the yard, raking leaves, or helping him organize his work bench. When implemented, this resulted in more tantrum than work done, and Mia was again, unfazed by the threat of this consequence.

Another complex component of our relationship was that as much as Mia slung anger and hate at me, she also asked for an overwhelming amount of reassurance and love. Our relationship was extremely complicated and emotionally confusing. I was her safe place for extreme anger and extreme need. When she told me she hated me and I should die, she'd reversely tell me she loved and needed me.

I got handwritten, heartfelt notes from her after volatile outbursts. Her intentions were loving, but the maturity and self-control necessary to follow through with her promises of change were not there yet. And to complicate things even more, once she had moved on from an outburst, she expected me to have moved on too and for us to be fine, which was not always the case. My feelings were hurt, and I sometimes needed time to heal, which would make her angry all over again.

"Dear Momma,

You know that I love you, don't you? I think that deep down inside, you know it, but right now you don't. I am so sorry, for real. I know that most times I'm not sorry but I am. I have a huge heart, and I wish that the nice girl inside would come out more often than the mean, ugly, and stupid girl that is out now and most times. I feel awful for what I did, and I try my hardest not to. Like in the car all those times that I stopped only for like a minute I actually tried to stop. But I just couldn't. It is so hard for me and that is bad. I know that all these mean and hurtful words hurt. You give me everything I need, and then I treat you like crap. I will try as hard as I can to be better. I love you more than anything.

Mia"

She relied on me to help her find physical and emotional calm, to reassure her she wouldn't throw up, and to help her cope with anxiety. My unconditional love that she used and abused was one of the most difficult challenges I had as Mia's mom. I felt the hurt and the exhaustion, but also a pull to meet her needs, to help and comfort her, to always be there for her, and you become necessary to her everyday existence.

Then there is the time you invest in your child. You love them so much their struggles become all-consuming. Mia's mental health continued to monopolize my focus. My days consisted of weekly therapy appointments, daily reassurances, positive reinforcement plans, dedicated homework hours, and any activities I needed to stay with her at. Ty and Zoe grew up playing in doctor's offices, tagging along to practices, and often entertaining themselves while I attended to Mia. I continued to neglect my needs, and I hardly noticed as the divide widened between Gary and me. There was less arguing, each of us now familiar and comfortable with our roles and robotically going through the motions of carrying them out, but there was also less meaningful connection.

To this day, though I believe you do what's necessary as a family unit for each member as needed, there are times I look back and feel guilty about the lack of time and attention Ty and Zoe got from me. Don't get me wrong, they turned out great. They are well-adjusted, kind, independent, and wise humans. There is no bitterness toward me. I know they are okay. Ty has reassured me that he holds no resentment and remembers me being very present for him while Zoe admits she doesn't remember much of those years. Perhaps that's her personality or her mind's way of protecting her. But it doesn't stop the sneaky claws of mom guilt from digging in at times.

Middle school had been a hard adjustment, requiring lots of work from Mia, myself, and her teachers to keep her progressing, learning, and successful. She was doing it but with plenty of guidance and assistance. Stomachaches were still an issue as was her aggressive personality at home, but academically, eighth grade threw us for yet another loop. I talked with her therapist because I was concerned she was starting to fall behind again. I knew the transition to high school the following year would be even more difficult if we could not figure out what was going on and revise our approach to helping her succeed. Gary and I were still unsure if Mia was simply lazy and unmotivated or if she was avoiding hard work and skirting responsibility.

But what if we relied only on our assumptions, and it turned out she had learning issues? I still thought it was a possibility and pushed for Gary to consider it. "What if Mia is not just uninterested? What if she's not making excuses or taking the easy way out? She was a really good student when she was much younger. What if we assume she's just goofing off when really, she's been struggling to learn this whole time? I think we need to find out once and for all. If it is laziness, then we'll know better how to handle it. But if it's something else and we miss it, she'll struggle for the rest of her school career," I said, working to persuade him. He agreed it couldn't hurt to get her tested, and we should look into all possibilities.

Her therapist suggested a neuropsychological evaluation and connected us with a facilitator she trusted. The evaluation would take place over a day of testing to evaluate Mia and how well her brain was working. The areas she'd be tested in included reading, language usage, attention, learning, processing speed, reasoning, remembering, problem-solving, mood and personality, and more.

Before the testing was scheduled, I needed to have a few of her eighth-grade teachers fill out a report detailing Mia's behavior both socially and academically while in each of their classrooms. Her math teacher described her as being more distracted during class. They stated she was social and had friends but didn't seem to fit in as easily. She was more impulsive and goofier, where her girlfriends were not as much anymore.

Her science teacher noticed Mia had become more distracted, was unorganized with homework and note-taking, and often needed to be reprimanded for not paying attention during class. And her language arts teacher wrote that Mia was distracting to others in his class because she liked to talk and goof around instead of doing her classwork. He also reported that, like in science, her note-taking was often sloppy, and she had become unorganized in class. All three teachers praised her for being hardworking and eager to please, but they also noticed signs of anxiety, especially about test taking.

The day of the evaluation, Mia was nervous and, as expected, pissed off at me for making her participate. It was an eight-hour day with a one-hour break for us to have lunch. I could not be in the room with her, making her anxiety worse.

"I already have a stomachache! What if I throw up?"

"I'll be out in the waiting room the whole time, so if you really need me, you know I'll be there," I said.

She and the clinical neuropsychologist performed a variety of "thinking games" like looking at pictures, drawing, and putting together puzzles. They also worked on specific tasks that involved solving math problems, sight-word reading, and spelling skills. Gary and I agreed, whenever we received the results, regardless of what they showed, we would present them to Mia as a gauge. This was not a "you are smart" or "you are dumb" evaluation. It was a tool to help her learn better and more easily. It would help us and her teachers learn how to best teach her according to how her brain processed information, hopefully making school less overwhelming.

I was anxious for Mia during her testing. It was a long day of a lot of information. It would be overwhelming and taxing, and I was proud of her for walking into that room alone, knowing how scared she was. There was a part of me that wanted to sit with her, help her, and make her feel more reassured and safer. But I also knew this was going to be positive and good for her. Through the struggle, she would succeed, whatever the results. And for me, I wanted an answer. I wanted to stop guessing at why school was hard for her. I wanted Gary and I to stop clashing over why she got the grades she got and the lack of effort she applied to her schoolwork.

When we finally got the testing back, the answers I had been looking for were laid out clearly in black and white type. Overall, testing showed my daughter to be a wonderfully average student. And average was perfect. It was exactly where she should've been. But more detailed results—the ones of greatest help—showed some areas of struggle.

For instance, testing revealed as an eighth-grader, Mia was reading at a sixth-grade level. It showed it was extremely difficult for her to identify the main theory of a story or summarize written text because she couldn't retain the information. This was exactly why her note-taking was awful and why she resorted to goofing off in class. If she couldn't keep up, she got distracted. Distraction led to talking and goofing around. Plus, how can the material be interesting when you aren't able to comprehend it?

The math testing showed when she could write out her work, she did well solving problems. The ability to write out the steps of a process and see them mapped out helped her get to the correct conclusion. But as performance expectations increased and content became more challenging, she couldn't keep up with the rest of the class.

I am so grateful we had the financial means, referral, and foresight to have that testing done. It gave us clarity. Mia was not in fact, lazy, but truly struggling. It was no wonder she didn't pay attention in language arts. She couldn't read like the rest of her peers. She couldn't keep up. She felt stupid and often lost. We now understood why she scored poorly when asked to summarize content for a social studies report. She was unable to. We finally had clarity and were able to provide her with help. We met with her teachers and school principal, bringing them into the loop so we could work together and have strategies in place to help Mia succeed.

For language arts, it was suggested that I read the assigned books alongside her—each of us having a copy—so we could talk through every chapter. I enjoyed the time with her, which was often spent in the car or in her room. She was curious and engaged, not angry. My heart was so happy to finally see her grasp material that had been complex before. I would explain portions of text she wasn't understanding and got to hear her say, "Oh! That's what she meant? I get it now!"

Her language arts teacher would require Mia to write out book reports like her classmates, a task she needed to practice, but then he'd also discuss the content with her one-on-one knowing she was better at recalling information through verbalization. He did the same with tests, having her take a paper version first along with the other students but, if she did poorly, he would meet with her to go over the answers she got wrong. She could more clearly articulate her thoughts and ideas when speaking as opposed to writing them out.

For math, we found a tutor to "preteach" concepts Mia's teacher provided him with so she could get a head start on comprehension. We worked on "prestudying" for tests, reviewing small pieces of information over longer periods of time to better retain the content.

Mia was given "preferential" seating in the classes where she struggled most. She was given a desk at the front of the room and closest to the teacher so as to eliminate as much distraction as possible and offer her direct contact for asking questions. Her teachers proposed the seat as a reward for being a star student, not a punishment.

We finally had some answers.

What a blessing to finally get some answers in an area of life where Mia struggled. Clarity led to better understanding, more grace, empathy, and finally, action. It allowed us to have more conversations with her and her teachers, raising awareness, and made room for planning. I had no idea at the time how much I would end up needing to feel that sense of control with regard to school because back at home, I would soon find my world turned upside-down, and it would become ultimatum time.

LOVE HARD TIPS
How to Find a Neuropsychologist

1. "Your pediatrician, a therapist, other parents, or the school may have recommendations.
2. Sometimes, the child's school or the board of education can make a recommendation or provide an evaluation.
3. Your insurance company may also provide you with a list of neuropsychologists in your area who are in network.

Reasonable Questions to Ask When Determining If a Neuropsychologist Is a Right Fit

1. What's involved in a neuropsychological evaluation? Even if you know, it's good to hear the explanation. Do they explain themselves clearly and fully?
2. How long does an evaluation take, and how much does it cost?

3. How do you work with parents, the child, and—if pertinent—the school?
4. How long does it usually take to get a report after the evaluation is complete?
5. Do you include educational recommendations in your report?
6. Do you participate in IEP meetings at the school" (Golden and Tomb 2023).

CHAPTER ELEVEN

———

I don't think balance is ever achieved in the full sense of the word. Life is more like a juggling act, spinning plates in the air, allowing some to drop, and picking them back up or adding new ones when the timing is right.

—CANDACE CAMERON

I've spent four years spinning the plates and trying to be everything to everybody. Parenthood, wifehood, faith life, appointments, housework, field trips, friendships, volunteering, meals, grocery shopping, laundry, yardwork, therapies, and extracurricular activities were a part of my daily activities.

Well, get a broom and dustpan because things were about to get messy.

Plate one crashed to the floor when we "aged out" of our wonderful therapist. She was the woman who had been my ally since Mia was in first grade and who I relied on to help her succeed. Their relationship became strained. Now at fourteen, the more Mia was required to take responsibility, the more resentful she became. She was defensive and uncommunicative during sessions and eventually refused to go altogether. It was a joint decision, but sad nonetheless, that I needed to start looking for someone new for us. To me, it was like the loss of a family member. Mia and I would go on to work with a few other therapists over the years, but I would never find one I shared such a close bond with.

Plate two came crashing down early fall when Gary was diagnosed with a rare autoimmune disease, transverse myelitis (TM). TM is "the inflammation (swelling) of the spinal cord. Inflammation can damage or destroy the fatty protective substance that covers nerve fibers. This damage causes scars that interrupt the communication between the nerves in the spinal cord and the rest of the body" (MS 2023). Symptoms often occur within hours or days of when the pain starts and include loss of balance, muscle spasms, difficulty walking and breathing, sensitivity to temperature and touch, burning and pricking skin sensations, and extreme fatigue.

It began with pain between his shoulder blades in August. By September, my husband, who prided himself on being an active father, corporate powerhouse, and competitive athlete, found it difficult to walk up the driveway or shower on his own without falling. He went from endurance waterskiing, regular running, and pick-up basketball games with coworkers to being unable to jog, walk up a flight of stairs, or do a single push-up. He could not work, sleep, and some days, could not get out of bed.

Mia was fourteen, Ty was twelve, and Zoe was ten. After years of long hours and a fierce dedication to work, Gary was just starting to enjoy more flexibility in his schedule. Time freedom to reassess his priorities and find a better work-life balance. He became more present in all areas of our family and relationship. He was more involved with the kids—volunteering to coach basketball, baseball, and softball teams. He paid more attention to Mia's mental health and her care. He empathized more, listened more, and supported me more. We both became more intentional with the health and needs of our marriage, spending extra time together whether it was at games or on dates, which was healing.

We were slowly bridging the gap that work, kids, and mental health created in our relationship when the rug was pulled out from under us. And though I would not wish transverse myelitis on anyone, Gary's diagnosis and long-term treatment would end up connecting us on a much deeper level and strengthening our relationship in ways we didn't know were possible. Sometimes, when you are forced to slow down and start over, you are able to see clearer the truly important things in your life. Your focus goes from broad to precise. And you no longer waste time on the unnecessary.

Got that broom? The year of 2014 brought with it transverse myelitis, and the year of 2016 brought us another autoimmune diagnosis. At Mia's sixteen-year physical, and after reading an eye-opening book called *Grain Brain* by David Perlmutter, I finally insisted she have bloodwork done to test for an intolerance or sensitivity to gluten.

"Doctor, I recently read that a person's gut health can directly impact their mental health. I'm wondering if some of Mia's anxiety or aggressive behavior might be because of the food she's eating, and I'd like to have her tested," I told her pediatrician.

She responded quickly, "Do food intolerances run in your family?"

"No, at least not that I'm aware of."

"Well then, it's really not necessary as it's often hereditary."

"That may be true, but I've been wanting to do this for a while, and I'm asking you to schedule the labs. I will pay out of pocket if necessary. This is important to me."

Parents, trust your gut and advocate when you feel moved to.

Mia's tests came back positive for celiac disease, "an auto-immune disease that's triggered by consuming gluten and results in damage to the small intestine. When a person with celiac disease eats gluten, the immune system sees gluten as a threat and attacks. However, it ends up damaging the villi of the intestines, which help to digest food. Damaged villi make it nearly impossible for the body to absorb nutrients, leading to malnourishment and a host of other issues" (Beyond Celiac Team 2023). Our pediatrician called me, shocked.

"Well, Deb, we got the lab results back, and Mia's not sensitive to gluten. She has full-blown celiac disease. I would've never guessed! I will have my nurse send you some information in the mail and the name of a nutritionist."

After her positive test, Gary, Ty, Zoe, and myself were tested, too, which was when we discovered Zoe's allergy as well. Her symptoms were milder and once again missed. She suffered from fairly regular but mild headaches, and we'd simply increase her water intake. She also suffered stomach aches and frequently vomited from what we assumed were numerous bouts of the stomach flu. Looking back, I'm sure it was due to gluten and not a virus.

It proved to be a life-changing discovery—and a lightbulb moment for some of Mia's behavior and symptoms over the years. After her diagnosis and the elimination of gluten in her diet, Mia grew seven inches in one year. The chronic psoriasis patches on her ankles and shins cleared up, both common indicators of celiac disease. As reported by Mayo Clinic Staff members, "the inability to absorb nutrients due to Celiac Disease might result in weight loss, irritability, short stature, delayed puberty, and neurological symptoms, including ADHD" (Mayo Clinic Staff 2021).

It also helped with her stomachaches because now, when she would get one, we had a possible reason.

"Mom, my stomach is hurting. Am I going to throw up?" she'd routinely ask.

"Let's think about what you ate recently. Do you think you might've eaten any gluten or maybe eaten something that was cross contaminated?" I could now distract her with this alternative.

"You know, your stomach is in the process of healing, so it might still hurt sometimes."

Minimizing the chance she had the stomach flu and replacing it with a valid but less scary possibility that it was her celiac disease helped to give Mia some control over her anxiety.

I do wish that we would've discovered her celiac disease much earlier, but our pediatrician's wheelhouse of knowledge was limited at the time about the connection between food and our brains and body. And honestly, there actually were logical reasons for some of Mia's symptoms. She was always the shortest and smallest by many inches, but both Gary and I were late bloomers. My father-in-law had psoriasis, so that explained why Mia did. Her stomachaches were due to the anxiety she was plagued with.

I was grateful for the diagnosis and the connection made between Mia's diet and health. But I was lost as to what came next and where I should start with changing our lifestyle amidst the busyness of our lives. We were parenting three active, athletic kids who played multiple sports year-round. They were enrolled at two different schools, which meant my morning drop-off and afternoon pick-up took an hour each way. Add in practice drop-offs and pick-ups, and I could easily be in the car for four or more hours simply shuttling kids.

We were also in the thick of research and treatments for Gary's autoimmune disease. Trips to Johns Hopkins Hospital and the Mayo Clinic, numerous doctor and specialist visits along with wellness practitioners and holistic healers. In the two years since his diagnosis, he continued to battle the disease, and he was working diligently with an amazing personal trainer to recover his balance and keep the strength he had regained after months of terrible but necessary steroid treatments. I hated the disease, but I loved how it brought us together, working as a team to find ways of adapting to our new normal.

We were desperate to find answers, symptom relief, and solutions for his nerve pain, muscle atrophy, and constant physical discomfort. Reiki, acupuncture, massage, food elimination, supplements, and cryotherapy were a few of the things he tried. He was on a strict, ultra-clean diet, which meant planning and prepping his meals took me time and attention. Our hope was that we could reduce his joint inflammation by eliminating common trigger foods. We knew there was no cure, but we prayed often for a remission of sorts.

And now, I was also cooking gluten-free. Gluten is a protein found naturally in wheat, barley, and rye and common in obvious foods such as bread, pasta, cookies, and cakes. However, I would find that many surprising products contained gluten, such as ice cream and sprinkles, lip balms and lipsticks, sauces, toothpaste, candy, gum, juices, and even the glue we lick on envelopes.

The overhaul of my kitchen and home was expensive and extensive. I had to learn what to cook, how to cook, and where and how to grocery shop quickly. I literally came home from learning of my daughter's diagnosis, stepped into my kitchen, and realized she could no longer eat 90 percent of the food I had, nor could she ever again eat at the fast-food restaurants I'd come to depend on for convenient meals on our busiest days. I had to clean my entire kitchen—counters, cabinets, drawers, pots, pans—to avoid cross-contamination and then ensure it remained clean after I made each meal. I needed to educate the girl's school, the parents of her friends, and our own friends and family to make sure meals and treats they offered were safe. I scheduled meetings for us with the nutritionist our pediatrician recommended to help navigate our new normal, and I worked to find a gastroenterologist for their future care.

Through it all, I was still navigating Mia's mental health. Home life freshman year remained the same, with regular tantrums, outbursts, and verbal attacks. School life, however, proved to be a positive experience both academically and socially. We chose a private Lutheran high school where her graduating class size would be forty students. It was the perfect fit. The school was small, inclusive, and helped immensely with her anxiety during the transition from middle school to high school.

She received one-on-one help from her teachers per the testing we had done, and accommodations like extra time and separate classrooms so she could walk around, take short breaks, and ask questions as needed while test taking. A quiet classroom intimidated her and was more distracting than a room full of activity. I received amazing support and regular updates from her school counselor and teachers. She was also able to participate in any extracurriculars she wanted and found success in volleyball, field hockey, basketball, soccer, softball, and even performed in a musical.

Now, sophomore year, Mia was still doing well academically but struggled socially. Some of her friends broke off into smaller groups, leaving her unsure of where she fit and who her people were. She chose fall field hockey over volleyball, and though she found she had talent and it was fun, it was intimidating starting over with a new team. There was a lot of transition and insecurity, which led to bigger problems at home. If possible, her fuse was even shorter, and she was more disrespectful. She regularly lashed out. Blowing me off with, "What's your problem?" or "Relax!" when asked to do homework or a chore. If pushed, she'd fly into a rage, physically shaking with intense anger, scratching the ground, her forearms, or a chair she might be sitting on. She'd impulsively throw things, sometimes at me, consumed with an anger she didn't know how to process.

Ty and Zoe kept their distance, unsure of her mood but fairly certain it would be bad. Gary and I were working to defuse two to four blowups a night. He was back to work with reduced hours, so I often dealt with two before he even got home when we'd then join forces for additional ones.

The first time your beautiful child screams, "I'm going to kill myself" while sitting on the edge of her open window with her legs dangling outside, you're paralyzed with fear. It's serious, devastating, and takes your breath away. You thought you'd heard it all and survived but this… this brings you to your knees. I'd sit with her, emotionally reassuring, empowering, and loving her. I talked through her feelings, asked her questions, and offered help.

As the anger left her body, she would then cling to me like the little girl she once was. "I'm sorry, Mom. I didn't mean it. I wouldn't kill myself. Don't stop loving me. I'd never hurt myself. I'd never want to be away from you. You are the best mom in the whole world," she'd plead. The next day, I was on the phone with her therapist and psychiatrist, making them aware of what happened and scheduling emergency appointments.

The second time comes as a gut punch as well. But maybe this time she threatened to call the police or social services on you because you took her phone away. You hold her, reassure her, wrap her in love. "I didn't mean it. I was just really angry. I would never call the cops. I don't ever want to be away from you. I don't want another mom. I love you. I'm sorry," she'd say, filled with remorse.

Even the third time, I'd play the mind game with myself that she didn't mean it the times before, and probably not this time either but, what if? It was too high a gamble, so once again, I would give her the reaction and attention. But I saw the pattern. Similar to her rage, the threats were impulsive and extreme. And as they became more frequent, I started to spend less time reassuring and more time making her aware of the damage her threats could do.

"I'm sorry, Mom. I would never jump out the window! You know I don't mean it, right? I just say it because I'm angry. And I wouldn't call social services. I don't want a different mom or a different house. I love you. Do you believe me?" she'd plead when sorry and contrite.

"Mia, you know I love you. It hurts me when you say things like you want to die or you want to live somewhere else. But I need you to know that you *cannot* keep threatening to jump out the window or call social services because those are extremely serious statements. If someone heard you say them, someone who doesn't know you say things you don't mean when you're mad, they could take you away. You could be forced to go to a hospital for threatening to kill yourself. And if you called social services saying you hate your home, they could remove you and put you in a foster home or child protective services while investigating us. Is that what you want?"

One night, after an argument, while Mia was in her room doing homework and I was back in the kitchen cooling off and cleaning up dinner, I got a call from a good friend of mine whose daughter was one of Mia's best friends at the time. Her daughter and mine had been texting, Mia having typed, "I hate it here so much. I hate my parents. I'm going to kill myself. I'm so mad." Her sixteen-year-old friend was terrified and wisely went to her mom with the conversation.

My friend was upset with the threats but also upset that Mia put all that concern, fear, and responsibility on her own daughter. I felt terrible for her daughter, for mine who still had no concept of the impact her words had and what they could cost her, and for myself, embarrassed and ashamed, feeling once again like a bad mom who couldn't control her child. You don't say, "Oh, she's only kidding. She says it all the time when she's mad. She's not actually going to kill herself, so don't you worry." There's no way to explain six-plus years of behavior, parenting efforts, and love in a phone conversation. There's only validating, apologizing, and reassuring her in ways you are able and staying silent when there are no words.

Once off the phone, I went to talk with Mia. I was so upset that she exposed herself and me. She brought our mess out for others to see thereby giving them permission to chime in. When I got to her room, she was still on her phone, and she was calm. I sat down across from her on the bed.

"Your friend's mom just called me. Any idea why?" I asked.

Barely looking up, "Nope," she responded, uninterested.

Okay, let's try this again.

"Put your phone down and look at my face, Mia. What did you tell your friend tonight while you were mad?"

She thought for a split second, "Nothing."

Oh, for crying out loud.

"Mia, I know you told her you were mad and wanted to kill yourself! She told her mom, who called and told me."

Her eyes shone with acknowledgment but also defiance.

"Your friend was really scared!"

"I can't believe she told her mom! I didn't even mean it. I was just super mad. That is so stupid!"

"We've talked about this, Mia. Your words are powerful. They carry meaning and consequences. And people can't see inside your head or heart when you say things. They don't know you don't mean it. So, they believe what you say."

Mia was still mad but also starting to realize that this was bad—really bad.

"I know you were angry. I believe you didn't mean it. But how scared do you think she was? How scared would you be if one of your friends told you they were going to kill themselves? Of course, she should've told her mom. And, of course, her mom did the right thing by calling me. But now, it's out there. Her mom wants to know how we plan to handle this. How we are going to help you. She asked if you should be hospitalized."

Things just got real.

"I don't want to go away! I was really angry, that's all! I'm really sorry," she said, her voice filled with fear and desperation.

We talked for a long time. I put restrictions on her phone and involved her therapists the next day who had been in the loop all along. The two girls repaired their relationship, but unfortunately, that was the beginning of the end of my friendship with the girl's mom. She eventually decided she didn't want her daughter influenced by mine, nor did she want her daughter carrying the burden of Mia's mental health struggles and over-the-top emotions.

I needed more help managing Mia than her therapy and medication offered, and I craved a break from her emotional needs. Our family unit needed an escape from the angry, explosive environment our home had become. Mia needed greater help managing her anger, treating her family with respect, and appreciating the love and privileges she was given. I didn't want to be numb anymore. Numb to the threats and outbursts. Numb to the insults. Numb to the anxious pleas for reassurance. And unfortunately, numb to gestures or words of love she offered. I was tired of always waiting for the other shoe to drop. I hated the mom and person I had become. We had tried everything but our last resort, which was something suggested to us by Mia's psychiatrist twice over the years, but we refused. The move I was so afraid and hesitant to make.

It was time for the ultimatum. Mia finally needed to change her behavior, or we'd send her away.

LOVE HARD TIPS
What to Do When Your Child Threatens to Kill Themselves

1. "If your child threatens to harm themselves, never ignore or dismiss them, even if you feel like they are trying to manipulate you or to garner attention.
2. Although you may think your child is trying to get attention, being dramatic, or attempting to manipulate you, it's important to seek help from a medical professional. This is not normal behavior. Do not try to deal with it alone or dismiss their suicide threats as teenage angst.

3. Talk to them about it, listen to their concerns, and ask questions about how they've been feeling.

   a. Simply start by asking if they are okay, how they've been feeling lately, and how they've been doing overall. It may be uncomfortable to talk about mental health and suicide, but talking about it can help your child to get the support they need.

   b. Follow their lead and give them the time and space to respond to you. Sit quietly with them and respect the silence. Don't interrogate them with multiple questions or accuse them of trying to manipulate you.

   c. Try to find out if there was a significant event that occurred that may have caused them to feel this way. Encourage them to share with you what happened and express that you want to talk about it.

   d. Validate their feelings and avoid minimizing their mental health issues. Paraphrase what they are saying and listen intently. Show that you're trying to understand from their point of view. Do not tell them to get over it or that they're just being sensitive or overreacting.

   e. Ask open-ended questions so that your child can't respond with a yes or no; this gives them an opportunity to share with you more thoroughly.

   f. Avoid telling them what to do, or giving advice or solutions to their problems, especially when they haven't asked for it. This can come across as dismissive as though you're shutting down the conversation.

   g. Show you are concerned for your child and you care about them. Tell them you don't want them to harm themselves.

h. Provide reassurance to your child by telling them they are not alone and you are going to help them through it all.

i. Talk to them about options for getting help for their mental health problems and gently suggest they try it.

j. Tell them you love them no matter what.

4. If they are not willing to talk to you, ask if there is a trusted adult they would feel more comfortable talking to like another family member, coach, school counselor, pastor, teacher, family doctor, or therapist.

5. If you sense your child is in immediate danger or self-harm is already occurring, do not leave them alone. Remove things in the home that can be used to harm themselves, such as medications, weapons, and guns. Seek medical assistance as soon as possible" (Chan 2023).

CHAPTER TWELVE

We have to teach people how to treat us, negotiate and renegotiate our boundaries, especially with the ones we love the most.

—ALEXIS JONES

My family was hurting. The unit itself had been repeatedly injured and now needed closer attention than what I had been giving it. For years, my focus was Mia. It wasn't bad. It was necessary. I didn't ignore Ty or Zoe. I didn't love them less. But because they required less of my attention, they received less. When you have a child with special needs, whether physically, mentally, or emotionally, your family is structured differently. Roles are defined. Certain behaviors are normalized. You learn to have more patience, more sensitivity, and more tolerance. Your family is not less than or more than anyone else's. It's simply unique. And every member matters.

The fighting, yelling, and threats were a lot—too much. They'd now gone on for too long, and everyone, even Mia, needed a change of scenery. I didn't want her to forever ruin the fragile relationships she still had with her brother and sister. I didn't want Ty and Zoe pushed so far that all they saw and remembered of their older sister was conflict. She had so much good to give, and I was afraid at some point, they would no longer offer her the chance to share it with them.

And I needed perspective. I needed a break from her rage so I, too, could remember the love.

The summer before Mia's sophomore year, when spending time with a mom friend visiting from Florida, I casually mentioned something about Mia being a challenge. I recounted an incident that had been hard. I was guarded and vague but felt safe. My story led to a deeper discussion as I learned my friend had struggled while raising her oldest daughter too. Our girls demonstrated similar behaviors, and I found such freedom in talking with another mom who understood.

"Your daughter seems to be doing well now. And you all seem to have a good and loving relationship. How did you get here?" I asked.

"It's taken time. And it's still not perfect. We have moments. But years ago, after trying everything we knew to try, we learned about a faith-based camp in Missouri. We chose to send Avery one summer," she offered.

"How did she handle going away? I can't imagine Mia being able to do something like that."

"She hated it. She hated us. Putting her on the plane for camp was one of the hardest things I've ever done, but I knew I was doing it out of love. And I prayed it would be healing for her and for our family."

"How did she do?"

"It was hard at first, but she figured it out. She's gone two more times since. Her sister went twice and our youngest, Lexi, will be going this year. It was a really good experience."

I recounted the conversation with Gary, feeling the flutter of hope.

"I spent some time talking with Jackie this past weekend. She told me all about a camp they sent Avery to when they were really struggling to parent her. What do you think? I know it would be super hard for Mia. She'd be terrified and hate us. But Avery was angry and scared, too, and ended up having a great time and even went back! It was a turning point for their family. Even our psychiatrist has suggested for us to take time apart. Compared to the wilderness camps he's offered, this would be way better. I'd feel better sending her here. It would be hard for me but, I'm all out of ideas on what to do," I said.

Gary and I started doing some research. The camp had been around for over ninety years and was committed to giving kids opportunities for adventures, responsibility, fun activities, and personal growth. There were reviews, testimonials, and payment plans. That, along with the praise it was given by our friends, made this sleep-away camp our newest parenting strategy.

"Hey Mia, remember me telling you how I talked with Miss Jackie a few weekends ago? And how she told me about that camp her daughter Avery went to a few years ago. The one where she zip lined and jet skied and did some rock climbing. Her sister Lexi is actually going this coming summer. You met Lexi up north." I brought up the camp, testing the waters.

"Umm, yes, I remember her. Lexi was super nice," Mia replied uninterested.

"I looked up the camp online the other day. Just to see what it offered. It looks really fun. I actually wish they had a camp for adults. I'd sign up to try a bunch of the activities they offer," I continued. This was not going to be easy.

"Dad and I were talking about maybe you going next summer too. We could sign you up for the same week or weeks Lexi is going even. So, you'd know someone," as I talked, I gained confidence in my presentation.

"What? You want to send me to camp? Like, send me away? No way! You don't even love me! I knew it!"

"We do love you. So much. But you're not happy here. You say it all the time. Don't you think about being somewhere else sometimes? Getting a break from us?" I didn't want her to turn this into us not loving her.

"There is no way I'm going to camp! I hate you!" and she stomped out of the room.

Not the way I had wanted it to go, but at least the idea was out there.

At her next therapy appointment, and without her in the room, I ran the idea by her psychiatrist. He was completely on board, reminding me camp was not a bad place. Lots of kids went and actually had fun. It would be very difficult for her, but he reminded me she was not giving us much choice by continuing to verbally attack us.

A week later, Gary and I sat with her and talked over the camp idea once again. "I know you don't want to go to camp. But I also know you have not been working very hard to change the way you talk to and treat any of us. Our home is supposed to be a safe place, and it's not feeling very safe these days. Here is what Dad and I have decided. If you spend this next school year working hard to be nicer, more respectful, more kind to Ty, Zoe, Dad, and me, and we actually see and feel change, you do not have to go to camp. I'm not looking for you to behave perfectly. We all lose our temper and get mad. But you need to try a lot harder, stop swearing at us, stop calling names, and stop making fun of your siblings. If, however, you don't try, you don't work on it in therapy, and you continue as you have been, then you will be going to camp. Do you understand?" I was trying to be clear but loving.

She was a good kid who, I believed, was strong enough at this age to start exercising more control. She was capable of treating us nicer, as she did with so many other people in her world. Friends, teachers, and the parents of friends always saw her kindness and sweetness. It was time for us to see it too. I'm sure she didn't believe we'd follow through. Remember, she didn't respond to future rewards or consequences. And any time camp was brought up, she swore she'd never go.

The school year went by with us frequently, but casually, reminding her what was on the table. Nothing changed, so we mailed in our down payment. This would actually not be Mia's first time away from us. She had done a weekend trip with her class in eighth grade and two trips—one out west and one to New Orleans—with our church youth group. I knew it would be scary, but I also believed she was capable.

As her sophomore year came to a close, and we hadn't seen or felt any change, we delivered the news.

"Mia, we just wanted to remind you of the plan. You were going to work on your behavior to avoid camp. Do you think you've been any better?" I asked.

"I tried to be nicer. I tried not to scream at you guys. Whatever," shoved in a corner, she was shutting down.

"Well, things have not been better. We'll give you some time to prepare, but we're going to sign you up for the August camp dates so you can be with Lexi. I will also get you set up with a gluten-free meal plan, and sometime this month, we'll pick the activities that you'd like to do." It was time to be consistent and follow through.

"I hate you! I will hate you forever if you make me go to camp! Why did you even have me if all you want to do is send me away? You don't love me! If you loved me, you wouldn't make me go to a stupid camp! You must love Ty and Zoe better. That's why you want me gone. Because they're perfect. I hate you all!" she screamed as she ran up to her room.

Summer leading up to camp was hard. It took all of me not to go back on our decision and let her stay home. I wanted to remain in the familiar instead of following through on the devastatingly hard. I came to realize as much as she depended on me, I actually had come to depend on her. I depended on our rituals and routines, and on monitoring, diffusing, and redirecting her emotions and outbursts. Her needs gave me jobs and purpose every day. As much as they consumed her, they had actually come to consume me too.

Her mood was all over the place. One minute, she'd be screaming she hated me and the next apologizing and pleading with me to forgive her so she could stay home from camp. One day, she didn't care if she was going to camp, and the next, she was obsessed and terrified about being away from me. And through it all, she obsessed. "What if I'm homesick? What if I cry the whole time? What if I get a stomachache? What if I throw up? What if I'm scared? Who will help me?" she'd ask repeatedly. And the true answer was, I didn't specifically know.

I know I said camp was for the benefit of our family. It was the break I felt we all needed. But there was one other reason I chose camp, which was college. It was two years away, and Mia had made very casual comments about maybe wanting to go away to school and live in dorms like her friends were talking about doing. I was surprised but encouraged. I knew a move like that wasn't realistic at the time, but I didn't want to disregard the idea. She needed to practice. She needed to dig deep into her toughness and discover what she was capable of. She needed to find out if she would break or survive.

She had seen glimpses of her strength in the three previous trips. Each time, she left with fear and anxiety but returned home proud of herself and more confident in her capabilities. I wanted normalcy for her. And not any other kid's normalcy—Mia's normalcy. I wanted her to, in two years, go to college because *she* wanted to go. To live in the dorms if *she* wanted to. I wanted her to know she could rise above her fear of throwing up and mainstream with other kids because, inside *she* wanted it. I wished for her opportunities to try things and see things, and be who she was fully meant to be despite her anxiety and OCD.

And it would only happen if my little bird was pushed from the nest and able to use her own wings. I would never push her if I didn't believe she could handle it or know without a doubt I could catch her if something happened. Her mental health had been a cage, keeping her from being the person I knew she could be and wanted to be. At sixteen and nearing adulthood, it was my job to empower her. To teach her she could do hard and uncomfortable things. She was strong, powerful, and capable.

I also knew Gary and I needed this time to focus on us for two weeks. In the past few years, we have made big progress reconnecting. But the diagnosis of transverse myelitis, though bigger picture brought us together, also completely changed our relationship. I took on the role of caretaker, and he lost his identity altogether. At work, he had been respected for his quick wit, brilliant writing, and confident, almost cocky stage presence during presentations. Now, he had trouble finding his words and remembering people's names. Where he had been an active athlete, he now lacked balance, stamina, and coordination. Steroids left him irritable, moody, and bloated. He was ashamed of his limitations and of no longer being the man I married.

"I'm sorry I can't help with the yard or the house. I feel so useless. I watch you take care of everything." He was often wracked with guilt. "I went to work today for a couple of hours, and someone walked in and asked me if I was better because I looked so good. Meanwhile, my back was killing me where the lesion is, sitting in my chair aggravating it, and my feet felt like they were set in blocks of concrete, the skin on my arms burned, and my hands kept cramping up while I was trying to type. No one can see all the things wrong, so they assume I'm fine. It's just embarrassing." There were many people close to us who would question the existence of his disease over the years simply because they couldn't see any outward "proof." Suggesting Gary was being dramatic or making his symptoms up. It was heartbreaking and an eye-opening realization as to who we could depend on for support.

I'd get so mad and protective. "Well, they're an idiot! Who would think you'd fake having a disease? Did you choose, in the restaurant last month, to take out our table when your legs locked up and you fell into it trying to sit down? Do you choose to be breathless when you walk up six stairs? Do you choose to fall in the shower? Do you choose to have regular brain and lung scans to check for lesions? Are we talking about building a wheelchair-accessible house in the near future, in case you have a relapse, for shits and giggles? I'm so sorry you have to entertain people who are insensitive."

It would be good for the two of us, without me managing Mia, my mood mirroring her ups and downs, to be together. It would be great to laugh and talk, go on dates, for me to be fun and open, and for life to be a little lighter.

The day to leave for camp came, along with tears and resentment. We had decided Mia and I would drive the almost ten hours together with one overnight stay along the way. Gary would hold down the fort at home and besides, he tended to trigger her, and she was already on edge. The ride was horrible. There was no laughing, only pain both felt and spoken.

"Which bunk do you think you want in your cabin?" I asked.

Silence.

"You signed up for a basketball clinic, which should be fun. You played well last season. Your teammates will be impressed."

Silence.

"You know I love you. I'll write to you and send you packages. This is really hard for me, Mia because I'm going to miss you a lot. You're a piece of me, and I'll be counting down the days until I can come pick you back up."

"Well, if you loved me so much, you wouldn't be making me go to camp! I'm going to have a terrible time, and I'm never going to talk to you again! I will hate you forever!" she shouted.

Okay then, I chose to go back to silence.

The next day, we tackled the last few hours of the trip. "Mom, I'm so scared. I really don't want to go. I'm sorry I yelled at you yesterday so much. I'm so nervous. My stomach hurts. Am I going to throw up? Please don't make me do this. I don't think I can." Mia was struggling badly. Her eyes filled with panic, and tears streamed down her face. My heart physically hurt. Her pain was mine.

With a wavering voice, I reminded her, "You are so strong Mia. I know you will be okay. You will make friends, and you will meet a counselor you like, and they will reassure you. The time will go faster than you think, and all of sudden, it'll be time to go home. I love you so much, and I'm so proud of you. If anything happens, I will drive back down and get you." Words I meant wholeheartedly but knew wouldn't cut it.

When we pulled up to the gates of the camp, we were greeted by super happy counselors singing, dancing, and excitedly greeting each car pulling in. I rolled down the window.

"Hi, and welcome to camp! We are *so* excited you're here! What's your name?" the sing-songy girl asked.

"Mia," she said, barely moving her lips.

"Hi, Mia! You're going to have so much fun! What cabin were you assigned?"

She directed us to the appropriate lot, where we parked, and then navigated our way to the sign-in table and luggage drop-off. Mia followed me closely, eyes big as saucers trying to take it all in while completely overwhelmed and stimulated. She and I went to the tram stop, where kids were being picked up and taken to their cabin to meet other campers and counselors. And apparently, that was where our journey was to end. Another happy counselor told me cheerily it was the end of the line for parents.

I panicked. Wait, wait. I'm not ready. I need to talk to someone about how special Mia is, what to watch for, how to reassure her. I need to see more of the camp so I'm reassured and familiar. I want to see where she'll be sleeping and eating. I want to meet her bunkmates. I need to spend more time with her before saying goodbye. This is my kid! She's scared! I can't just leave her here yet, all ran through my head as my heart started to race. And her eyes. Her big, beautiful, trusting eyes pleaded with me. All the brokenness, all the anger, all the hurt, all the numbness was covered in love. A mother's love. An unconditional love. An "I'll die for you" love.

Looking back, I know the camp was super smart in hustling us off quickly, as much for the parents as the campers. Long goodbyes are never easy. They were making us rip the Band-Aid off in one quick pull. A counselor approached us, and it was time. Tight hugs, lots of "You can do this," and "You won't throw up," and "I'll miss you so much," whispered in her ear. She started tearing up, and I knew I had to go. One last "I love you," and I turned around, walking quickly to the car. By the time I looked back, she was gone.

I sobbed. Ugly, body-wracking, can't-catch-my-breath sobs. I had to pull over. Wait. Clear my eyes. Take deep breaths. Get back on the road. Pull over again. Get composed. Resume the drive. The crying and grief lasted a while. Sometimes it overwhelmed me, and sometimes it was simply an emptiness. Part of my heart was back at camp and the hole left, massive.

The definition of irony? Me believing once Mia was at camp and out of the house, I would breathe easier. Find peace. Feel more carefree. Enjoy the emotional break. The joke was seriously on me! I was glad for the respite from daily fights and outbursts, don't get me wrong. And Gary and I did make time for us. But remember, a piece of me—even if it was a bit jagged and rough—was hundreds of miles away. I worried every day. Phone calls and emails were not allowed. I waited every day for a letter. I had sent several of them. I waited some more. Did she connect with her camp counselor? Did she like her bunkmates? Did she get the top or bottom bunk? What did she think about the activities? Who was reassuring her? Was her stomach hurting? How was the food?

The not-knowing was awful. I scoured the camp's website daily for photos of her, finding a few here and there. She was smiling. But I analyzed them, and I worried some more. Ironically, I got a letter from her a few days before we were set to drive down and pick her up. It was filled with anger at me, as well as sadness and betrayal. She had written it on the third day of camp, and it broke my heart. I prayed her experience and feelings had changed since then.

Camp was coming to an end, and Gary and I made the drive down to Missouri to pick up Mia. I could not wait! I craved my daughter like an addict craves their next fix. She was part of me and had been gone for fourteen long days. Gary and I had so much fun on the way, stopping in cute towns, listening to our favorite playlists, and talking without interruption. "I can't wait to see her! To hug her! Do you think she had fun? Do you think she'll be excited to see us or mad?" I wondered aloud with the windows down and my hair blowing in the warm wind.

"I'm excited to see her too. I've missed her and prayed every day she was okay and that she made friends. I hope she had fun, but I suppose we'll know when we see her," Gary replied.

Once we arrived and parked, we were directed to the meet-up area, where kids and their parents were reunited. We waited alongside other expectant families, all peering over each other in hopes of seeing their kids. And we waited. And waited. The whole time, we watched other moms and dads hug and kiss their kids. Finally, I saw Mia. She was aloof, hesitant, and taking her time. As soon as she reached us, I hugged her tightly, spilling over with words of affection, but she was stiff, stoic, and emotionless.

"Oh my gosh, do I love you! How are you?" I joyfully gushed.

"Hi. What," Mia responded bitterly.

"What do you mean, what? I'm so happy to see you! I missed you every day! How are you?" I said, full of love and soaking up her face.

"It's not a big deal. I'm fine. I'm going by my friends," she replied. Gary barely got a hug himself before she walked away.

Our reunion was brief before we moved to the welcome program, where Mia found her camper friends. We stood in the back, nursing our wounded hearts, as the program began. One of my favorite things besides physically touching her again was watching as the counselors and campers celebrated my daughter. All she had accomplished. They highlighted her strengths, spoke about her gifts, shared what they liked about her, and gifted her with a specific bible verse chosen just for her.

We took videos and clapped, beaming with pride. But I knew. I knew things were off. I sensed her anger. I was disappointed. All this time, I had been counting down the days until pick up. Knowing she started angry but praying she ended up having fun. Expectations will kill you. We paid the price. The entire nine and half hour ride home. The first couple of hours, she didn't speak. Then, she started sharing.

"Just so you know, I hated camp! I cried every day. I threw away your letters. I hated the counselors, and most of the activities were boring. I hate you both for making me go, and I will forever! You should've just left me there," she said with so much anger. She wanted to hurt us the way we hurt her. It certainly wasn't the reunion I envisioned, but nonetheless, I had my girl back and was hopeful for the days ahead.

It's seven years later, and Mia will now fully admit camp was actually really fun, and she made some great memories and friends while there. "Oh, I loved camp. I made so many friends who were different, and they liked me. The food was amazing! We had bonfires and bible studies. I actually felt really close to God at times while I was there. I did miss you a lot, and I was really, really angry when you picked me up. There was no way I was going to admit that I had fun though. I wanted to punish you. And I was mad," she said with a smile. "But I know now it was really good for me. I learned I was stronger than I thought and remember being proud telling my friends that I went and about the new friends I'd met," she finished.

This is the "why" we sent her, to show her and the world she was capable. She was strong enough. She was so much more than violence, worry, or anger. And she could handle anything—even really, really hard things. Ten years of the battle, and there was still more battle to be fought, don't get me wrong. But she'd always be worth it.

Raising kids is a marathon, not a sprint. "Each lap we take, we must keep our eyes focused on where we're headed. Not on the crowd or on the competition the world throws our way. And if you look over, you'll find me there. Feeling each stumble and celebrating victories with cheers. And I will remember the distance we've traveled as I pray for the time we have left to go. And I'll thank God every single day that motherhood is not a sprint" (Warren 2019).

LOVE HARD TIPS
Eight Benefits of Sleepover Camp

1. "Kids learn to be independent. When kids are able to successfully spend time away from parents, it can help them develop autonomy. Many kids come home from camp with increased self-esteem because they've had the opportunity to tackle new challenges on their own.

2. Children often have an opportunity to reinvent themselves. They may be shy at school but can become both popular and more outgoing at camp.

3. Kids have a chance to make deep connections. When kids live together, they have the opportunity to develop meaningful relationships with peers. Those who spend time away at camp frequently describe making lifelong friends.

4. Campers develop new skills. By trying out activities such as crafts, kayaking, and drama, kids have a chance to expand what they're able to do. Particularly for kids who may feel excluded from some activities during the school year, camps provide an opportunity to be included—and to hone in on skills kids may not know they have.

5. Kids learn to respect and appreciate others' differences. By living together, kids learn how to get along with peers who may be different from them. At the very least, campers become better at negotiating social interactions.

6. Kids learn about responsibility at camp. Tasks are assigned, and there are expectations to keep the cabins clean. There is also peer pressure to work as a team.

7. Children get used to living without electronics. This gives kids the opportunity to learn how to enjoy free time

without staring at a screen. It's a great chance for kids to read a book or to seek out a friend for a nature walk or just to chat.

8. Camp can help the whole family combat cabin fever. Kids and parents get a break from each other, which reduces stress and can be very revitalizing" (Greenberg 2017).

CHAPTER THIRTEEN

After all the surrender, after all the grace, after all the strug-
gle you have had to face, there comes a time when you know.
Finally, it's your time to shine.

—KELLY MARTIN

The white gown hung on a hanger from the top of her bedroom door. When I walked past it, I was flooded with warm
memories. I saw her in the white gown she wore for her bap-
tism. Then the white dress she wore at my brother's wedding
when she was two. Flash forward to the white dress she wore
for senior prom. My throat tightened, and my heart leaped.
We did it.

High school graduation day was here.

Mia lettered in five sports over her four years. She was team
captain twice and on homecoming court. She graduated with
a 3.3 GPA, earning her a significant academic scholarship to
the university she had been accepted to. She worked with her
school counselor and teachers to achieve those grades, and we
found tutors to help her tackle the ACT. She had a boyfriend,

a summer job, and a thriving social life surrounded by really good friends. She not only did it. She crushed it!

It was the beginning of June, and the high school gym was hot and packed on graduation day. Sweat ran down my back. The paper fans we waved were inadequate. The bleachers filled with other expectant parents, grandparents, family, and friends of the kids about to walk across the stage. Many of their kids like my own, having gone through grade school, middle school, and high school alongside Mia.

When her row was excused, and she looked back to find me before heading to the front, my heart stopped for a split second. Her face was brilliant, smile wide, and eyes shining. She radiated joy and love. I wanted to shout, "Hey everyone, look at her! That's *my* kid!" The girl who had struggled hard to study, to test, to acclimate, to succeed, to blend in while standing out. She was about to walk across the stage right alongside her peers and receive a diploma. My breath quickened as my cheeks flushed and my eyes became teary. A sappy smile painfully pasted across my face. My heart was full. My job was not done, but man, I felt validated. All the prayers, all the therapy, all the accommodations, and all the time, attention, effort, and love shone bright through her smile.

And now, she was headed to college. My kid, with her anxiety, worries, insecurities, and fear of throwing up, was going to college. But not just that... wait for it... she was going to live in the dorms with roommates she had yet to meet. I was amazed. I saw the beauty of God's hand in Mia. We had worked so hard for so long for this independence and for her to mainstream. For Mia to be, in her own words, like "everyone else."

Though she had come very far, that summer before college came with challenges. This was a huge change. Lots of unknowns brought on lots of worry and insecurity. What helped was that, unlike camp, this was Mia's choice. She wanted to be like her friends going off to college. She truly wanted to experience the freedom and independence of dorm life.

We strategically chose a local school, Concordia University Wisconsin, for several reasons. One, it was only twenty minutes from home, giving her the reassurance that worst case scenario, we could come to get her. Two, it was small, and she would feel less lost on campus while having access to more one-on-one attention if needed. Three, she knew other kids from her graduating class who were enrolled too, including one of her best friends. And finally, it offered the major she was interested in, interior design.

"Mom, I'm really scared to be away from you. I mean, I want to go to college, and I want to live in the dorms. I want to tell people that's what I'm doing, just like my friends. But I'm so afraid of getting sick. What if I throw up? And I'm afraid of being lonely. And I'll miss you. If I need you, you would come, right?" she'd ask nervously.

"I know this is super scary, and I also know you can do it. You are stronger than your fear. You're only twenty minutes away. If you need anything or need me to come get you, all you have to do is call. You'll have friends and roommates. Sure, it will be hard, but it will also be fun. Remember, you can call me anytime." I'd reassure, trying to ease her anxiety enough to move forward with planning and packing.

The change that happened toward the end of Mia's senior year of high school was pivotal. She had cut back on therapy quite a bit since getting back from camp sophomore year. She managed okay her junior year. But senior year, with college looming and maturity occurring, she took ownership of her therapy, choosing to start again, and this time on her terms and by her own choice. This is when the magic happens, moms. When your child is no longer going and participating because they "have to" and instead because they "want to." She didn't want to live scared. She wanted to be able to handle college. And she was finally ready to own her journey.

"I'm so nervous about going to college, but I also really want to," Mia said one day.

"Okay, I think it would help if you found someone to talk with about it. Someone you could then see even when you're at school if you needed to," I suggested.

She thought about it briefly before agreeing, "I think you're right. Will you help me find a new therapist?"

With maturity and age, she became more aware of behaviors that were holding her back. When she'd fly out of control in anger, she now recognized that it was inappropriate and would be left feeling embarrassed and ashamed. Her dependency on me for reassurance made her feel self-conscious and childish. She asked more often, "Why did God make me this way, Mom? Why am I this angry? I hate that I say things I don't mean. Why do I have to be on medication and see a therapist? Why am I so afraid of throwing up when no one else is? Sometimes, I wish I was never even born."

"Stop right there, Mia. God only makes good things, and you are good. You've just had to work harder than others. Instead of asking, 'Why did God create me with mental health struggles that have made life hard,' I want you to change the narrative. I want you to ask, 'Who will I help because I understand mental illness, and how will my struggle change the life of someone else?' I believe I was created having OCD so that when God gave me you, I would notice it in you and understand. I would know how to help you," I replied. That can be said for any one of us who battles a demon or shortcoming. We can choose to use it as an excuse or flip the script and find the meaning and purpose behind our struggle.

We worked together to find her a new psychiatrist and therapist. On our first visit with her psychiatrist to discuss her history and current symptoms, Mia was, for the very first time, given a diagnosis. In his professional opinion, he believed she suffered from OCD, anxiety, and ADHD. Mia found hope and peace in finally knowing what she was dealing with so she could work to devise a plan for management and healing.

While Mia worked that summer to develop a relationship with her new therapist and address her anxiety and fear of throwing up, I did my best to be her hype squad. Many of my mom friends shared tears and heartbreak over their kids leaving for college. Not me. No way could I be weak. No way could sadness show. We had worked too long and too hard to get to this point in life. My unhappiness, trepidation, or insecurity would only translate to Mia.

All summer long, I cheered Mia on, trying to get and keep her excited about this new adventure. Upbeat about all the opportunities she would be offered. Optimistic about the friends she would meet and how fun dorm life would be. At the same time, I continuously reminded her that we were only a car ride away. My feelings? I kept them tucked tightly and safely away for quiet moments alone.

Like the afternoon, reality sucker punched me in my rarely relaxed gut. Catching me off guard the week before Mia was to leave. I happened to walk past her bedroom, like I did thousands of times before, and caught a glimpse of her open suitcase packed full of, well, full of her—her clothes and shoes, her toiletries, her photos, and trinkets.

It stopped me in my tracks as I watched her pack up her existence. That suitcase, and the packing boxes strewn across her floor, made me catch my breath, and my heart exploded. I quietly and quickly hurried to my room, shut the door, and allowed the tears to come. Covering my mouth to quiet the sobs that racked my body. Crying tears of sadness that she was leaving and I had to let her go, mixed with tears of joy for the very same reason. She succeeded! After years spent fighting the mental health battle, she had taken control. She was reigning in the monster. And though it was a bittersweet moment, I felt triumphant.

College drop-off went surprisingly well. We spent the day moving her in, meeting her two roommates and their parents.

We went for lunch and walked around campus, joining a freshman orientation dinner. She was distracted by organizing her things, visiting with existing friends, and meeting new people. There were no tears and very little worry.

Like camp drop-off, our college goodbye was quicker than expected. It was getting late in the day, and Mia needed to attend a dorm meeting. When her hall manager came to get the girls, it was our cue to leave.

"Okay, bye Mom," she said, coming in for a hug. "I'm nervous. I'm not going to throw up, right?" she whispered.

"Nope, you're not going to throw up. I am incredibly proud of you. You have fun and call me later if you need to. You're going to be just fine, Mia," I said, hugging her tightly and kissing her cheek. She kissed me back and went to Gary.

"Bye, Dad. Thanks for helping me today. I love you," she stood on tiptoes and said softly in his ear. Gary was emotional. Leaving, even though she'd be close to home, and knowing it would be really hard for her.

Through tears, he told her, "I'm really proud of you, Mia. I love you very much." Quick kiss and she hustled out the door already laughing and talking with her new friends. Gary and I walked down to the car, quiet. I felt at peace. I believed she could do this, and she would thrive. She was exactly where she was meant to be.

As expected, Mia struggled from the first night spent on campus. Homesickness hit hard and would trigger her fear of throwing up. And then there was dorm life. She shared a room, public showers and toilets. There was very little privacy. People stopped by all the time. Common spaces were loud and crowded. People got sick. Meals were only available during specific times of the day, unlike at home where the kitchen was open twenty-four-seven. Her gluten-free options were tasty but limited. And then classes started, and homework. She needed to develop and stick to a schedule while finding the right places to study. It was a lot of change all at once, and for Mia, trying to adjust was more angst than ease.

It's not uncommon for kids to struggle and especially those who struggle with mental health. "Going to college can be a challenging time for many students. In addition to separating from their families for the first time, students must learn to cope with academic pressure, lack of structure, live with people they don't know and take on adultlike responsibilities. Because of this, many college students experience a worsening of their existing symptoms. College is very different from high school, and because OCD symptoms often increase during times of stress and transition, it is not uncommon for OCD symptoms to flare" (Groundwork Counseling 2017). It was nothing we hadn't seen coming, but it was tougher to manage with phone calls.

And the phone calls did come. Mostly at night for reassurance and to talk. After the first couple of months of school, some of her friends started leaving campus on the weekends to go home. This would cut down on the social opportunities Mia was offered and what she was comfortable being a part of. That first year, she was apprehensive about going to parties off-campus, especially with people she didn't know very well. Therefore, she spent a lot of time alone in her dorm room. She didn't have a car, so she didn't have freedom. Her homesickness and anxiety spiked.

"Hi, Mom," Mia called one night.

"Hey Mia, how was today?" I answered from the bed as it was after eleven at night.

"I'm just really anxious. My roommates went home. And there's a house party, but I stayed back this time. So, I'm alone. I hate feeling stupid for not going, but the music is always really loud, and there's always a lot of people, so it's super hot. I get overwhelmed, and I get worried that the cops will come. That happened last weekend at someone's party, and three people got tickets. So now, I have nothing to do, and I know my friends are having fun without me. I wish I could just come home," Mia said.

"I'm sorry you're alone. Do you want me to come get you tomorrow? We could go to lunch." I'd offer, feeling miserable that she was stuck by herself. It became our routine that when her roommates or friends went home, I would pick her up if she wanted to come home too. It gave her a couple of days to decompress, but it also made going back more difficult.

We gutted out that first semester. Night after night, I'd coach her through the anxiety, reassure her she would not throw up, and tell her tomorrow would be better. She was still seeing her therapist regularly and taking medication. I saw her often, driving her to her appointments, bringing her home for dinner, or treating her to lunch. At the end of semester one, she asked to get a job off campus. The caveat being she would need to use our car and keep it at school. We told her if she got a job, she could take the car back to campus after winter break.

She got a job at an Italian restaurant as a server, which was another "Is that really my kid?" moment when she willingly chose, and was amazing at, a job that was hard work and required patience and grace for both polite and problematic customers. Her job had her driving past our house the days she worked, which meant she'd often stop over on her way back to school to say hi, see the dog, or grab food.

As months went by, her visits lasted longer and eventually led to sleepovers. I noticed the pattern. I encouraged her to go back to school while choosing my battles. She was, and still is to this day, my homebody. The child who spent so many years fighting us finally found peace in loving us. She felt most comfortable as part of our whole. The back and forth between school and home continued the entire second semester.

At the end of freshman year, Gary and I celebrated that Mia had indeed accomplished dorm living for an entire year, but admitted that it was probably not realistic going forward. We helped her pack up her room and moved her back home for the summer.

"Mia, what are you thinking about the dorms next year? Have you reached out to your friends to see if anyone has room?" I asked. Her two roommates from freshman year were not coming back to the dorms, so she needed to find new people to live with.

"Yeah, I asked a couple of my friends, but they don't have room. One girl said she was checking. I'll ask her again, but I don't know if I want to live on campus next year. It was really stressful, and I feel comfortable here at home," she admitted. After numerous discussions as a family and with her therapist, we decided it was in our best financial interest, and healthiest for her mentally and physically, that she live at home and commute to school during her sophomore year.

Not living in the dorm while also having a job and a car gave Mia the confidence and freedom necessary for her to remain social and involved with her friends on and off campus but on her terms. Her grades were good. She was completing assignments, passing tests, and showing up for class consistently. Sophomore year, she split her time between two campuses, one nearby and one in downtown Milwaukee, Wisconsin. She loved meeting new and different people, the vibe of downtown life, and the independence her major was affording her. Passionate about interior architecture and design, she was enjoying school and learning.

In her junior year, the pandemic hit, and life shut down. We had just moved into our new wheelchair-accessible house, a proactive transverse myelitis precaution we hoped we'd never need. Although I hated the virus, I loved having my kids and husband under one roof full-time. We played games, did puzzles, binge-watched shows, went for walks, tried new recipes, Face Timed our loved ones and attended church online on

Sundays as a family. Mia continued her therapy over Zoom and found comfort in the familiarity of our new normal that would end up lasting a whole lot longer than anyone had originally anticipated.

During her senior year, Mia took a leap of faith and moved into an apartment with a friend from college. After two years at home, growing and working on herself, she felt ready and excited. She wanted her own space and to try independent living once again. From choosing decor, to hosting parties, to personalizing her room, she loved apartment living and her independence.

Throughout her four years of college, Mia made new and wonderful friends while learning to let go of those who no longer fit in her life. Those who could not accept her for who she was and those who threatened to bring drama, anxiety, or heartache to her fragile but healthier mental state. She was working hard on herself and learned to protect what she had achieved.

College graduation day was another milestone that all those years earlier, I couldn't imagine being in the cards for Mia. That is the power of unending love, continuous prayer, therapy, medication, faith, grace, forgiveness, grit, and perseverance. Here was my beautiful, strong, mental health warrior of a daughter receiving her degree in four years, majoring in interior architecture and design with a minor in event management and hospitality, and working an internship at a local home staging company that would lead to a paid position after graduation.

This time, unlike four years before, I didn't cry. In that moment, I was overcome with joy and immense appreciation. As she walked across the stage to the cheers and applause of family and friends, I remembered and silently said thank you to all the wonderful people who helped her get to this very place. This included her teachers, her principals, so many coaches, friends, family, therapists, doctors, camp counselors, scout leader, babysitters, and employers. I was overwhelmed with gratitude.

It takes a village to raise not just a child but a mom. I was blessed to have numerous family members and friends surrounding me over the years. They were specifically put in my life at the right time and place. They showed up when I desperately needed support, loving Mia unconditionally. They prayed for and with me and breathed belief and hope into me when I was at my most hopeless. I believe lots of people close to me will be surprised by the accounts in this book, never knowing the extent of Mia's struggle or the depth of my overwhelm, embarrassment, and exhaustion. I often wonder, as I look around a gym or restaurant, who else is hiding in plain sight like I did for so long.

I believe that on my worst nights when I would crawl into bed admitting to Jesus that I wasn't strong enough or I couldn't make it through one more day and pleading for help, every time I asked, He granted me grace. This grace included a morning without anger, an unexpected note of encouragement from a friend, a hug from my husband, a beautiful sunrise, or a call from my mom. He was always there with me and Mia, guiding us and allowing us to experience struggle while also giving us lifelines when needed. He was the ultimate example of what it means to truly love hard.

I've heard it said that behind every big moment are thousands of small actions it took to get there. It's not the big moments we should hope for. It's the courage and discipline to do the small stuff. Don't worry about winning the Super Bowl… just get the first down. Mia's joy and success and our healed relationship took many small actions to achieve the big moment of today. Had we focused our eyes only on the desired result, we would've thrown in the towel a long time ago and missed out on the blessing of life now. Instead, we took it one day, one hour, and one minute at a time. We are finally able to look up to the sky, arms raised, screaming, "We made it," and enjoy the rest of the ride.

LOVE HARD TIPS
Managing OCD in College

1. "Seek therapy and digital support early on. The sooner you get a sense of on-campus and online resources, the more support you'll enjoy as you navigate the ins and outs of college. Then, when new difficulties arise, you'll already have an advocate in your corner.
   a. Many college students report success with exposure and response prevention (ERP) therapy, which involves gradual exposure to triggering situations. Some people also benefit from cognitive behavioral therapy (CBT), which involves identifying and correcting problematic thoughts or behaviors.

b. In addition to one-on-one therapy, consider joining a support group if it's available. It can help to know that you aren't alone. The students you meet in your support group can give you valuable insight into available resources or symptom management strategies.

c. If on-campus support groups are unavailable, try a virtual alternative. Many excellent groups can be found through social media or even be enjoyed via videoconferencing apps. Discussion boards can also be a great source of comfort if you prefer a more anonymous approach.

2. Work on sleep hygiene. OCD can both trigger and be exacerbated by sleep deprivation. To encourage quality sleep, opt for as regular a schedule as you can arrange. Try your best to fall asleep and wake up at approximately the same times each day. If you have a roommate, work together to develop a basic schedule for quiet time and lights out. When you're ready for bed, set your smartphone aside and read a book or listen to soothing music instead.

3. Practice mindfulness. A growing body of research suggests that mindfulness-based interventions may play a valuable role in managing OCD, especially in stress-heavy environments that tend to exacerbate the condition. Mindfulness can be integrated into several aspects of your daily life as a college student. For example, if your school's fitness center offers yoga or meditation classes, consider signing up. Otherwise, simply dedicating a few minutes each day to deep breathing can make a difference.

4. Record your symptoms. Your OCD symptoms may shift over time—and with them, the management tactics that work best. Awareness will help you understand which

aspects of the college environment tend to trigger OCD symptoms. A journal or smartphone app dedicated to recording symptoms may help. Consistency is key, but even occasional notes will give you a sense of emerging patterns. Take note when you observe:

   a. Obsessive thoughts or ruminations that interfere with your studying or social life.

   b. Unhealthy coping mechanisms, such as drug or alcohol use.

   c. Insomnia that you suspect is primarily driven by OCD.

   d. Compulsive behaviors that involve cleaning, counting, or checking" (Valentine 2021).

EPILOGUE

———

Life is like photography. You need the negatives to develop.

—ZIAD K. ABDELNOUR

It's a Monday morning. I lace up my black Nikes and head downstairs to our home gym, waiting for Gary to join me. The house is quiet. I select a playlist, and music fills the room. I turn on the TV and scroll through my options, finally settling on a full-body workout. And so begins what has become my morning routine.

In 2016, having lost myself to Mia's mental health and years spent taking care of my family, I was offered a lifeline that changed the trajectory of my life—fitness. At the time, I was uncomfortable with my body, stuck in unhealthy habits, and questioning what I had to offer my family, much less the world, when one of my closest friends became an online health and fitness coach. Knowing I was desperate for change, she asked me to join her. What began as a skeptical but supportive yes, led me on a path of self-discovery and personal growth. Exercise empowered me. Eating healthier became a labor of love, impacting me and my family. Being part of an online community of women found me friendship, support, and a place where I was noticed and valued. It was everything I had missed and craved, so I made it my job.

Had I not said yes that day in January, I would not have learned how to respect and accept myself. I learned that self-care is necessary, not selfish. I learned to delegate and draw healthy boundaries with my family. I remembered my love of and talent for writing, which would lead to this book years later. I helped other women find joy and confidence through wellness. I supported Gary on his fitness journey when gyms were shut down during the pandemic. I wouldn't have been able to show my kids that, at any time in life, you can start again, you can learn something new, or that being afraid is okay, and failing is when growth begins.

Gary is my best friend and biggest fan. We've weathered storms, and staying married is a daily choice, but it is one I will make over and over again. We laugh, we play, we fight, we cry, and we always come home to each other. He continues to manage transverse myelitis through exercise and diet. His symptoms are still present but far less debilitating. He competes in a cross-country ski race every year and is back to recreationally barefoot waterskiing.

Gary's daughter lives in New York and has blessed us with two amazing grandkids. Her partner has a daughter from a previous marriage, gifting us a third wonderful grandchild.

Mia loves her job with a home staging company and truly is amazing at what she does. There's something to be said about finding your passion. Where once she struggled to learn, she now embraces it—expressing herself creatively and confidently. She continues to work to manage her OCD and anxiety through therapy and medication. Her emotions will always be big. She loves hard, feels deeply, laughs loudly, and lives life with a passion and freedom that comes with being secure in who she is and what she expects.

Ty is loving life at the University of South Carolina. He will always be my sweet boy whose love language is physical touch. He is loyal, fiercely protective of those he loves, and ambitious. I am still a sucker for the twinkle in his eye.

Zoe heads to the University of Kansas this fall. She has grown into a strong, confident woman. She is adventurous and fun, reminding me a lot of her dad. She is also confidently quiet, sensitive, and funny. Her smile will light up the room.

Though I celebrate the strength and resiliency of my family, we will always be flawed—perfectly imperfect. And there is a rare beauty found in the rough edges that make us unique.

And so I will always,
choose to be deeply committed.
choose to compromise.
choose to ask for and give forgiveness.
choose to be vulnerable.
choose to see good.
I will always choose to love hard.

ACKNOWLEDGMENTS

My greatest desire in writing *Love Hard* was to tackle the complex subject of parenting a child struggling with mental health. I hope I have done so with the respect and love I intended and that it deserves. I believe too many people refuse to seek help because of shame and embarrassment. I myself was one of them. And there is still a stigma surrounding mental illness because more stories aren't told.

I'm thankful that God placed people in my life who've helped me survive, learn, grow, and thrive. I am here today, writing this book, because of your belief, love, and friendship. I'm also grateful for those who have shown Mia kindness and support over the years. Every one of you had a hand in helping her develop the confidence, security, and acceptance she has today. It is a gift to see her spread her beautiful wings and fly, free from the cocoon that was her mental health.

Mindy: Your friendship got me through years of parenting hell. From one stay-at-home mom to another, our phone conversations and emails covered everything from dirty diapers and sick kids, to mom life, marriage, and mental health battles. You laughed and cried with me. You listened to and loved me for over twenty-seven years. You saw Mia, loved Mia, supported and encouraged Mia. You have always been in my corner—my hype girl, my protector, my confidante. I love you.

Candy: You welcomed me that very first summer up north—the newbie alone with three kids, one being a real firecracker. You connected me with other women, so I had a network of friends, and you invited me into your circle. Over the years, as our friendship grew, you listened when I needed an unbiased ear, advised with tenderness and wisdom, and celebrated every milestone Mia achieved with me. To this day, the love and pride I see in your smile when you greet my daughter means the absolute world to me. I can't love you enough for that.

Robin: You were a gift later in the parenting journey. You allowed me to be vulnerable, raw, and honest about Mia. No judgment. No criticism. Just a glass of Pinot Grigio and a "welcome to the shit show" as we exchanged the ups and downs of raising kids. You love, love (not a typo, I intentionally said it twice because she loves her that much) my daughter and all my kids. But you truly appreciate the big, bold, beautiful woman Mia is today. Thank you.

Julie: I cannot forget that it was you who invited me to the Women in Faith mom's conference so many years ago. It was the moment I connected with another mom who was raising a strong-willed child of her own. It's where I first heard a mom's honest and raw account of the hard, the ugly, the sometimes shameful journey that parenting a child with mental health struggles can be. Someone else understood, and I was not alone! Through you and that invitation, I found hope, a renewed belief in God's plan, and the strength to stay the course.

Cathy, Paula, Kathy, Annie, Jamie, Lisa, and Heather: You planted the seed and then said yes to that long ago invite I put out to start a bible study with me in my basement. I wanted to work on my faith, but I was also desperate for friendship, connection, and a life raft to support me during the storm of Mia's mental health struggles. We never talked about what I was struggling with, not in full transparency, but all of you were that life raft. You buoyed me up by seeing me, appreciating me, praying with me, laughing with me, and giving me something to look forward to month after month. God gave me you for sustenance, and I am thankful to this day for the way each of you touched my life and the friendships we still have.

My BODi team: Many of you I didn't know before we met through this crazy but wonderful work-from-home job we said yes to. And now you are my people. You are the women who told me I had talent, I was important, and I was appreciated and worthy over years when my own self-belief was missing. You are the community that lifts me up, cheers me on, and wants me to see success. You have taught me so much. I love being your teammate and am so grateful for all of you.

To our First Immanuel Lutheran Family: For ten years, you worked with me to raise Mia. You cared for her, accepted her, taught her, but most of all, so many of you truly knew and loved her. You offered support and accommodations in the years she struggled. Thank you for the waived phone call fees, extra health room time, hallway hugs, bathroom passes, one-on-one attention, encouraging notes, secret signals, and so much more. Thank you for helping me raise her knowing the saving grace and love of Jesus.

To our Living Word Lutheran High School Family: From her guidance counselor and principal to teachers and coaches, you genuinely cared about Mia and worked closely with her so she would see success. You made sure she didn't fall through the cracks by noticing her, celebrating her, challenging her, and loving her. Thank you.

To the team at Manuscripts Modern Author Accelerator: Thank you for providing a platform to bring my book to life. Angela Ivey for being the very first set of eyes to read my story and for your help to make it better. Jordan Waterwash for saving me during citations. Allison Browning for your patience, guidance, and commitment to keeping me accountable and focused on the end goal.

My sister-in-law Julie: You were there for so many of Mia's milestones. You gave me the gift of peace of mind, as a new mom returning to work, knowing my daughter was loved, safe, and in the next best place to home while I was at the office. You and Joel loved her from the moment she was born, and your belief in her has never wavered. You have been a constant source of unconditional love and support, always there to cheer her on, advocate for her, or provide reassurance and encouragement. Thank you.

Grandpa and Grandma Mueller: I summered many years with the kids at our cabin up north. I loved the small-town feel, but the weeks alone were long and lonely without Gary to help manage Mia's emotions. You often stepped in. Hosting us for dinners, going to the beach, or watching the kids so I could have an hour or two of quiet. Thank you for the part you played in nurturing Mia's enthusiasm and love of the Northwoods and the comfort and joy she still gets at the cabin. I am grateful for your support back then and your unconditional love of Mia.

Kevin: What a gift to watch my baby brother as an uncle and godfather. The moment Mia wrapped her tiny hand around your finger, I watched you fall in love. Thank you for believing in this book and in me.

My dad: He never understood the anger and outbursts but always saw through them to who Mia was at her core—funny, athletic, beautiful, talented. His precious baby girl. He was so proud of every bit of her. I love the man he became the day he met Mia.

Mom—Gramma Sweet Pea: No words are adequate. You counseled Mia so many nights when I was emotionally unable to do it one more time. You prayed for me, listened to, and loved me when I was at my lowest and most desperate, always reminding me I was an amazing mom who was capable. And along with Dad, you willingly took on babysitting and the emotional turmoil it usually brought with it, so Gary and I could pay attention to and nurture our marriage through date nights and getaways. To this day, you remain one of Mia's most trusted and loved human beings. And for your overwhelming love and support of me always—as a daughter, wife, mom, writer, coach, and person. I learned how to love hard by watching you. You are a wise, strong, and resilient woman who I am proud to call my mom. Thank you.

K: For allowing me into your family and accepting me as your dad's wife. For being patient when I was acclimating to being a step-mom. For loving Mia, Ty, and Zoe as your siblings. Thank you.

Ty and Zoe: Two of my greatest blessings. Thank you for believing in me as an author and cheering me on every step of the way. I love that I get to be your mom.

E, Z, and R: Granny loves you.

Gary: You are the place I call home. Thank you for doing this life with me, for battling mental health alongside me, and for choosing me and our family every day. You have been my rock through this writing process. Holding me up, cheering me on, reading, and rereading every version and taking on more responsibility so I could focus and finish. Your praise, pep talks, and belief has kept me going and kept my eye focused on the prize of who our story might help. I love you always.

Mia: Thank you for letting me share your story, for trusting that I will do so with love and respect, for reading each version and giving me feedback, and for believing in me and our mission of helping others. One of the greatest gifts of my life is you, and I will always, always be proud to be called your mom. I still hate roller coasters, but I've loved the time spent riding with you. We did it, Meems!

Finally, I'd like to thank the very generous group of individuals who purchased a copy of this book during the presale. You are the ones who made the publication of this story possible. Thank you.

Abby Glawe, Aimee Wiley, Alyson Wagoner, Amy Hartwig, Amy Newman, Amy Schomann, Andy and Karen McMillion, Angela Harvey, Angela Wang, Angi Krueger, Anita Moyer, Ann Kovich, Anna Duerwachter, Ashley Knudson, Beckie Kruse, Beth Blessing-Foat, Bethany Dykstra, Brian Sterricker, Bridgette Frommell, the Buzzell Family, Candy Dailey, Carey Bartlett, Carolyn Sutter, Carrie Brooks, Casey Cohn, Casey DeGroot, Chad Kroening , Christina Araque, Christine Bonneau, Christine Mueller, Connie Kison, Cory Ampe, Courtney Ernst, Dacey Erik, Dana Casey, Darci Bandi, Darlene Stimac, Dave Draeger, Dawn Lesniewski, Dawn Riley, Dawn Walker, Deb Pietsch, Denise Kohnke, Donna Wolden, Doreen Krause, Ellen Mathein, Eric Koester, Erik Knudson, Fabiola Ramirez, Gale Taylor, Gary Mueller, Giovanna Caravella, Hannah Ramirez, Heidi Clifton, Heidi Fagre, Hervey and Goma Juris, Holly Kramer, J.J. Brojde, Jamee Belland, Jamee LeMonds, Jane Basten, Jane Brown, Janice Tank, Janine Brzezicki, Jayne Lang, Jennifer Humphries, Jennifer Criel, Jennifer Ellis, Jennifer Jurss, Jennifer Kachichian-Miller, Jennifer Kolsky, Jennifer Schaefer, Jenny Prom, Jessica Molisani, Jill Krueger, Jill McGuire, Jodie Landgraf, Jody Kelley, Joelle Lefevre, Joette Richards, Johnny Sprecher, Jolene Last, Jonna Pinion, Judy Langreck, Julie and Joel Knudson, Julie Schmid, Julie Witt, Karen McLain, Karen

Nennig, Karen Schaefer, Karri Spataro, Kathryn Kincaid, Kathryn Pahl, Katie Ferguson, Kayla Hill, Kennedy Kingston, Kevin Steltz and Suzanne, Kim Dobberfuhl, Kim Kroening-Weyker, Kim Marotta, Kim Moore, Kim Tweeden, Krista LeTourneau, Kristen Mueller and Em Card, Kristin Balistrieri, Kristin Maurer, Lacy Keepers, Laura Bauknecht, Laura Gainor, Laura Morris, Lauren Murray-Feller, Lauren Sutter, Laurie McGraw, Leah Ulatowski, Leslie Meyer, Linda Kurth, Lindsey Henning, Lisa Harsch, Lisa Kwiat, Lisa Liljegren, Lisa Manor, Lisa Newcomer, Lisa Ollmann, Lisa Ritt, Lori Helm, Luke Howard, Macie Palubicki, Mackenzie Lindmeyer, Maddy Pesch, Maria Rozek, Marie Judd, Mariela Fonseca Ruiz, Marissa Glinski, Mark Gerardot, Marlee Rawski, Marni Hebert, Mary Kircher, MaryLee Odem, Matt Molisani, Matt Willms, Meg Wienser, Megan Gerber, Megan Stahl, Meghan Willman, Melissa Lamm, Mia Mueller, Michelle Killian, Michelle Paape, Michelle Sobon, Mike Holicek, Mindy Dorff, Monica Darst, Nancy Kellner, Nancy Maciolek, Neva Moga, Nichole Haas, Nick Verbeten, Nicki Grob, Nicole Coombs, Nicole Kaiser, Nicole Valdez, Nora Brooks, Pam Dorsha, Pat Steltz, Patricia Dubitsky, Peggy Grabow, Peggy Houle, Penny Carter, Rebecca Walsh, Renee Ison, Robin Buzzell, Rochelle Steiner, Russell Golomski, Sandra Krueger, Sarah Anderson, Sarah DeCraene, Sarah Knuth, Shannon Fogarty, Shannon Stoker, Shari Ashley, Sharon Evers, Shawna Parsons, Sherrie Dorff, Sheryl Willms, Staci Belland, Sue Weeden, Susan Lenz, Susan Samz, Susan Simon, Tamarr Vollmar, Tammie Behling, Tana Myhre, Tania Dantas, Teri Watson, Terri Burmester, Theresa Schroeder, Tina Pegorsch, Tracy Gordon, Tricia Novak, Wendy Heintz

APPENDIX

CHAPTER ONE

Mayo Clinic Staff. 2022. "C-section." Mayo Clinic. June 16, 2022. https://www.mayoclinic.org/tests-procedures/c-section/about/pac-20393655.

WebMD Editorial Contributors. 2022. "Placenta Previa: Symptoms & Risk Factors." *Grow* (blog), WebMD. Accessed on June 15, 2023. https://www.webmd.com/baby/guide/what-is-placenta-previa.

CHAPTER TWO

Higgins, Erin. 2021. "C-Section Recovery Timeline and Aftercare." *Health Essentials* (blog), Cleveland Clinic. October 13, 2021. https://health.clevelandclinic.org/c-section-recovery/.

Karten, Michelle M. 2019. "Colic." *Nemours KidsHealth* (blog), KidsHealth. November 2019. https://kidshealth.org/en/parents/colic.html.

Kendall-Tackett, Kathleen. 2017. "How Cultures Protect the New Mothers." *Women's Health Today* (blog), Praeclarus Press. July 30, 2017. https://womenshealthtoday.blog/2017/07/30/how-cultures-protect-the-new-mother/.

March of Dimes. 2021. *Baby Blues after Pregnancy*. Arlington, VA: March of Dimes. Accessed on June 18, 2023. https://www.marchofdimes.org/find-support/topics/postpartum/baby-blues-after-pregnancy.

Morgan, Jamie. 2020. "5 Tips to Help Manage the Baby Blues—and When to Seek Help." *MedBlog* (blog), UT Southwestern Medical Center. March 10, 2020. https://utswmed.org/medblog/5-tips-help-manage-baby-blues-and-when-seek-help/.

O'Connor, Amy. 2023. "Cluster Feeding." *First Year* (blog), What to Expect. May 24, 2023. https://www.whattoexpect.com/first-year/breastfeeding/cluster-feeding/.

CHAPTER THREE

Alexander, Fo. 2022. "How to Prioritize Yourself First as a Mom Without Feeling Guilty." *Mama and Money* (blog). August 14, 2022. https://mamaandmoney.com/prioritize-yourself/.

Ladipo, Tonya. 2013. "Relationship Fairness: What a 50/50 Balance Means." *GoodTherapy* (blog), GoodTherapy. August 26, 2013. https://www.goodtherapy.org/blog/relationship-fairness-what-a-50-50-balance-means-0826134.

Mayo Clinic Staff. 2021. "Sleep Terrors (Night Terrors)." Mayo Clinic. April 23, 2021. https://www.mayoclinic.org/diseases-conditions/sleep-terrors/symptoms-causes/syc-20353524.

Pacheco, Danielle. 2023. "Night Terrors." *SleepFoundation* (blog). May 18, 2023. https://www.sleepfoundation.org/parasomnias/night-terrors.

Schilder, Donna. 2019. "Put Your Oxygen Mask on First." *Lead to Energize* (blog), Donna Schilder Coaching. Accessed on June 19, 2023. https://www.donnaschilder.com/articles/life-coaching-articles/put-your-oxygen-mask-on-first/.

CHAPTER FOUR

Deupree, Sidney. 2023. "CBT for OCD: How It Works, Examples & Effectiveness." Choosing Therapy. May 13, 2023. https://www. choosingtherapy.com/cbt-for-ocd/.

International OCD Foundation. 2023. "What Causes OCD?" International OCD Foundation. Accessed on May 30, 2023. https:// iocdf.org/about-ocd/what-causes-ocd/#return-note-67-1.

Johns Hopkins Medicine. 2023. "Obsessive-Compulsive Disorder (OCD)." Johns Hopkins Medicine. Accessed on May 30, 2023. https://www.hopkinsmedicine.org/health/conditions-and-diseases/obsessivecompulsive-disorder-ocd.

Manson, Mark. 2016. *The Subtle Art of Not Giving a Fuck.* New York, NY: HarperCollins Publisher.

Shea, Molly. 2021. "Try Greeting Your Anxiety with the 4 Rs." *Shine* (blog), The Shine App. June 21, 2021. https://advice.theshineapp.com/articles/try-greeting-your-anxiety-with-the-4rs.

Stulberg, Brad. 2022. "My O.C.D. Diagnosis Was a Blessing, until It Became Too Central to My Identity." *The New York Times,* July 3, 2022. https://www.nytimes.com/2022/07/03/opinion/ocd-mental-health-labels.html.

Wright, Stephanie A. 2022. "How to Stop Intrusive Thoughts When You Live with OCD." *Psych Central* (blog). August 4, 2022. https://psychcentral.com/ocd/how-to-stop-ocd-intrusive-thoughts.

CHAPTER FIVE

Cohen, Rebecca. 2022. "What Happens after a Miscarriage? An Ob-Gyn Discusses the Options." *Experts & Stories* (blog), The American College of Obstetricians and Gynecologists. June 2022. https://www.acog.org/womens-health/experts-and-stories/the-latest/what-happens-after-a-miscarriage-an-ob-gyn-discusses-the-options.

Jensen, Julie. 2020. "How Do You Heal a Broken Heart? Coping after Miscarriage." *Healthy Driven Blogs* (blog), Edward-Elmhurst Health. October 2, 2020. https://www.eehealth.org/blog/2020/10/coping-after-miscarriage/.

Marks, Hedy. 2022. "Pregnancy and Antidepressants." *Grow* (blog), WebMD. November 28, 2022. https://www.webmd.com/baby/pregnancy-and-antidepressants.

Moore, Fernanda. 2017. "How to Heal after a Miscarriage." Modern Ghana. Accessed on June 26, 2023. https://www.modernghana.com/lifestyle/10399/how-to-heal-after-a-miscarriage.html.

Santiago-Munoz, Patricia. 2018. "Cervical Ripening Methods When Induction Is Part of the Birth Plan." *MedBlog* (blog), UT Southwestern Medical Center. January 30, 2018. https://utswmed.org/medblog/cervical-ripening-techniques.

Valeii, Kathi. 2021. "What Is a Fetal Doppler?" Verywell Health. Accessed on June 20, 2023. https://www.verywellhealth.com/fetal-doppler-5119457.

CHAPTER SIX

Pruess, Angela. 2022. "10 Anxiety Symptoms in Children that Most Parents Miss." *Child Behavior* (blog), Parents with Confidence. November 30, 2022. https://parentswithconfidence.com/anxiety-symptoms-children-parents-miss/.

Robinson, Jennifer. 2023. "What Is Emetophobia?" WebMD. May 15, 2023. https://www.webmd.com/anxiety-panic/what-is-emetophobia.

Saripalli, Vara. 2023. "Understanding Emetophobia or Fear of Vomit." *Health* (blog), Healthline. May 24, 2023. https://www.healthline.com/health/emetophobia.

Weiss, Elizabeth. 2023. "Raising a Child with Emetophobia: How to Cope with a Fear of Vomiting." *Parents,* January 6, 2023. https://www.parents.com/kids/health/childrens-mental-health/raising-a-child-with-emetophobia-how-to-cope-with-a-fear-of-vomiting/.

CHAPTER SEVEN

Abraham, Kim, and Marney Studaker-Cordner. 2023. "Anger, Rage, and Explosive Outbursts: How to Respond to Your Child or Teen's Anger." *Empowering Parents* (blog). Accessed June 4, 2023. https://www.empoweringparents.com/article/anger-rage-and-explosive-outbursts-how-to-respond-to-your-child-or-teens-anger/.

Hutten, Mark. 2013. "'Blind Rage' in Children on the Autism Spectrum." *My ASD Child* (blog), My Asperger Child. October 2013. https://www.myaspergerschild.com/2013/10/blind-rage-in-children-on-autism.html.

Young, Karen. 2023. "15 Things Kids or Teens Say That Could Mean 'I'm Anxious'—Where They Come From and How to Respond." *Hey Sigmund* (blog). Accessed June 4, 2023. https://www.hey-sigmund.com/anxiety-in-children-things-kids-say-that-could-mean-im-anxious/.

CHAPTER EIGHT

Gordon, Sherri. 2020. "How to Rediscover Your Sense of Self in Motherhood." *Verywell Family* (blog). August 2, 2020. https://www.verywellfamily.com/overcoming-pressures-to-be-super-mom-4164348.

Green, Julie M. 2016. "Helping Kids with Sensory Processing Disorder." *Today's Parent*, February 2016. https://www.todaysparent.com/kids/helping-kids-with-sensory-processing-disorder/.

Pratt, Michelle. 2023. "12 Tips for Overwhelmed Moms." *Safe in the Seat* (blog). February 27, 2023. https://safeintheseat.com/tips-for-overwhelmed-moms/.

Saranga, Vinay. 2019. "Why Your Child's ADHD Outbursts Are So Explosive—and Isolating." *Saranga Psychiatry* (blog). December 11, 2019. https://www.sarangapsychiatry.com/blog/why-your-childs-adhd-outbursts-are-so-explosive-and-isolating/.

CHAPTER NINE

Child Mind Institute. 2023. "Angry Kids: Dealing with Explosive Behavior." *Family Resource Center* (blog), Child Mind Institute. March 13, 2023. https://childmind.org/article/angry-kids-dealing-with-explosive-behavior/.

Fuller, Clifton. 2020. "Roller-Coaster Ride of Anxiety." *Clifton Fuller Counseling* (blog), Clifton Fuller Counseling. Accessed June 7, 2023. https://www.cliftonfullercounseling.com/blog/anxiety-roller-coaster-ride.

Halli, Christina. 2015. "What to Say to a Parent of a Child with Mental Illness." *Healthy Place* (blog), Healthy Place. March 29, 2015. https://www.healthyplace.com/blogs/parentingchildwithmentalillness/2015/03/what-to-say-to-a-parent-of-a-child-with-mental-illness.

CHAPTER TEN

Golden, Claire, and Meghan Tomb. 2023. "What Is a Neuropsychological Evaluation?" Columbia University Division of Child and Adolescent Psychiatry. Accessed on June 26, 2023. https://childadolescentpsych.cumc.columbia.edu/articles/what-neuropsychological-evaluation.

Love and Logic Institute. 2023. "Parenting with Love and Logic." Love and Logic. Accessed on May 24, 2023. https://www.love-andlogic.com/pages/about-us.

CHAPTER ELEVEN

Beyond Celiac Team. 2023. "What Is Celiac Disease?" Beyond Celiac. Accessed on June 19, 2023. https://www.beyondceliac. org/celiac-disease/.

Chan, Katharine. 2023. "What to Do When Your Child Threatens to Kill Themselves." *Family Education* (blog), Family Education. April 27, 2023. https://www.familyeducation.com/teens/ health/mental/what-to-do-when-your-child-threatens-to-kill-themselves.

Mayo Clinic Staff. 2021. "Celiac Disease." *Diseases & Conditions* (blog), Mayo Clinic. Aug. 10, 2021. https://www.mayoclinic. org/diseases-conditions/celiac-disease/symptoms-causes/syc-20352220.

MS (National Multiple Sclerosis Society). 2023. "Transverse Myelitis (TM) and Multiple Sclerosis." National MS Society. April 2023. https://www.nationalmssociety.org/What-is-MS/Related-Conditions/Transverse-Myelitis.

CHAPTER TWELVE

Greenberg, Barbara. 2017. "8 Reasons to Consider Sending Your Kids to Sleepaway Camp." *Wellness* (blog), *US News*. April 7, 2017. https://health.usnews.com/wellness/for-parents/articles/2017-04-07/8-reasons-to-consider-sending-your-kids-to-sleepaway-camp.

Warren, Jaclyn. 2019. "Motherhood Is a Marathon, Not a Sprint." *Motherhood* (blog), Her View From Home. March 23, 2019. https://herviewfromhome.com/motherhood-marathon-not-a-sprint/.

CHAPTER THIRTEEN

Groundwork Counseling. 2017. "Managing OCD in College." Groundwork Counseling. Accessed on June 23, 2023. https://

www.groundworkcounseling.com/ocd/managing-ocd-in-col-lege-specialized-ocd-therapy-orlando/.

Valentine, Keara. 2021. "Managing OCD in College." *NOCD Blog* (blog), NOCD. April 9, 2021. https://www.treatmyocd.com/blog/managing-ocd-in-college.

Made in the USA
Monee, IL
01 May 2025

16733848R00128